What people are saying about …

# *Crazy Love*

"Chan writes with infectious exuberance, challenging Christians to take the Bible seriously. He describes at length the sorry state of 'lukewarm' Christians who strive for a life characterized by control, safety, and an absence of suffering. In stark contrast, the book offers real-life accounts of believers who have given all—time, money, health, even their lives—in obedience to Christ's call. Chan also recounts his own attempts to live 'crazy' by significantly downsizing his home and giving away his resources to the poor. Earnest Christians will find valuable take-home lessons from Chan's excellent book."

**Publishers Weekly**

"In Francis Chan's unique style, and with an urgency that seeks to awaken a sleeping church mired in the comfort of middle ground, *Crazy Love* quickly gets to the heart of the matter and leaves you wanting more … more of the matchless Jesus who offers radical life for all right now."

**Louie Giglio,** visionary architect, director of Passion Conferences, and author of *I Am Not, but I Know I AM*

"Francis's life reflects authentic leadership tempered by a deep compassion for the lost, the last, the littlest, and the least. It's all because this man, my friend, is an ardent and devoted disciple of his Savior. In his fresh new book, *Crazy Love*, Francis peels back what we *think* the Christian life is, and guides us down the path toward an uncommon intimacy with Jesus—an intimacy which can't help but change the world around us!"

**Joni Eareckson Tada,** best-selling author and speaker

"In an age of religious phonies, spiritual apathy, and disheartening books suggesting that God is a delusion, *Crazy Love* shines like a glorious beacon of hope and light. If you're stuck in a religious rut, read this refreshing book. I found it eye-opening and soul-thrilling. Whether in the pulpit or on the page, Francis Chan effuses love for Jesus Christ and demonstrates practical ways to throw off lukewarm Christianity and embrace full-on, passionate love for God."

**Kirk Cameron,** actor and author of *Still Growing*

↓↑

crazy love

# crazy love

## OVERWHELMED
### BY A RELENTLESS
# GOD

## FRANCIS CHAN
### with danae yankoski

David C Cook®
*transforming lives together*

CRAZY LOVE
Published by David C. Cook
4050 Lee Vance View
Colorado Springs, CO 80918 U.S.A.

David C. Cook Distribution Canada
55 Woodslee Avenue, Paris, Ontario, Canada N3L 3E5

David C. Cook U.K., Kingsway Communications
Eastbourne, East Sussex BN23 6NT, England

David C. Cook and the graphic circle C logo
are registered trademarks of Cook Communications Ministries.

The Web site addresses recommended throughout this book are offered as a resource
to you. These Web sites are not intended in any way to be or imply an endorsement
on the part of David C. Cook, nor do we vouch for their content.

LCCN 2008922793
ISBN 978-1-4347-6851-3
eISBN 978-1-4347-6655-7

© 2008 Francis Chan
Published in association with the literary agency of D. C. Jacobson & Associates LLC,
an Author Management Company www.dcjacobson.com

The Team: John Blase, Jack Campbell, and Amy Kiechlin
Cover Design: Jim Elliston
Author Photo: Kevin Von Qualen, 2007

Printed in the United States of America
First Edition 2008

23 24 25 26 27 28 29 30
090309

*Heavenly Father, thank You for Your grace.*
*Your forgiveness is SO good that I struggle with believing it at*
*times. Thank You for rescuing me from myself and giving me*
*Your Holy Spirit. Your love is better than life.*

*To my best friend, Lisa,*
*for being a godly, gorgeous, excellent wife and mother*

# ACKNOWLEDGMENTS

Thanks to …

Danae Yankoski for all of the effort and heart you put into this book.

Don and Jenni at DC Jacobson and Associates for your encouragement and help.

Todd and Joshua for serving the church and college God has given us to lead.

My assistant, Sandy, for being a great helper and a cool old lady.

The members of Cornerstone Church for passionately pursuing God with me.

# CONTENTS

# FOREWORD

It is with great excitement and honor that I get the opportunity to introduce you to my friend Francis Chan. Francis is one of those rare people you come across in life who leaves you wanting to be better. You know, a better friend, a better neighbor, a better athlete (well maybe not athlete … I can take Francis in most things involving competition). But most important, Francis leaves you wanting more of Jesus. If you are around Francis for more than thirty minutes, you soon realize that he is a man with great vision and resolve for the mission of Jesus. Some might say that Francis is a bit of an idealist in thinking that one life can really make a dent in the world. But I would say that Francis is the ultimate realist. Meaning, someone who believes that God is really who He says He is and that the true reality of this life is to follow Him wholeheartedly.

The book you have in your hand, *Crazy Love*, may just be the most challenging book outside of God's Word you will read this year. (And for a few years to come for that matter.) The status quo and norms of the so-called "Christian" life that so many of us are used to experiencing are in for a shock! Isn't it interesting that in Acts 11, at the end of verse 26, it says, "The disciples were called Christians first at Antioch." What I find interesting is the simple thought that the Christians didn't name themselves. But rather, they were *called* (or named) "Christians" by those watching their lives. I wonder if it would be the same today. Could someone look at your life or look at my life and name me a Christian? A humbling question for sure.

*Crazy Love* is the perfect title for this book. When Jesus was asked, "What is the greatest commandment?" he responded with "Love."

> "Love the Lord your God with all your heart and with all your soul and with all your mind." This is the first and greatest commandment. And the second is like it: "Love your neighbor as yourself." (Matt. 22:37–40)

As Francis so brilliantly illustrates, the life that Jesus calls us to is absolute craziness to the world. Sure, it's fine and politically correct to *believe* in God, but to really *love* Him is a whole different story. Yeah, it's nice and generous to give to the needy at Christmas or after some disaster, but to sacrifice your own comfort and welfare for another may look like madness to a safe and undisturbed world.

I am challenged to the core by the pages you're about to read. I am excited that you are diving into this much-needed book. I encourage you to face up to the convictions of *Crazy Love*. I know your heart and spirit will be stirred again for your First Love.

—Chris Tomlin,
songwriter and worship leader of Passion Conferences

# PREFACE

*To just read the Bible, attend church, and avoid "big" sins—
is this passionate, wholehearted love for God?*
—François Fénelon, *The Seeking Heart*

We all know something's wrong.

At first I thought it was just me. Then I stood before twenty thousand Christian college students and asked, "How many of you have read the New Testament and wondered if we in the church are missing it?" When almost every hand went up, I felt comforted. At least I'm not crazy.

In this book I am going to ask some hard questions. They will resonate with what a lot of us feel but are generally afraid to articulate and explore. Don't worry—this isn't another book written to bash churches. I think it's far too easy to blame the American church without acknowledging that we are each part of the church and therefore responsible. But I think we all feel deeply, even if we haven't voiced it, that the church in many ways is not doing well.

I get nervous when I think of how we've missed who we are supposed to be, and sad when I think about how we're missing out on all that God wants for the people He loved enough to die for.

I haven't always felt this way. I grew up believing in God without having a clue what He is like. I called myself a Christian, was pretty involved in church, and tried to stay away from all of the things that "good Christians" avoid—drinking, drugs, sex, swearing. Christianity was simple: fight your desires in order to please God. Whenever I failed (which was often), I'd walk around feeling guilty and distant from God.

In hindsight, I don't think my church's teachings were incorrect, just incomplete. My view of God was narrow and small.

Now I am a husband, a father of four, and the pastor of a church in Southern California. Until just a few years ago I was quite happy with how God was working in me and in the church. Then God began changing my heart. This took place largely during the times I spent reading His Word. The conviction I felt through the teachings of Scripture, coupled with several experiences in third-world countries, changed everything. Some serious paradigm shattering happened in my life, and consequently in our church.

The result is that I've never felt more alive, and neither has Cornerstone Church. It's exhilarating to be part of a group of believers who are willing to think biblically rather than conventionally, to be part of a body where radical living is becoming the norm.

↓↑

This book is written for those who want more Jesus. It is for those who are bored with what American Christianity offers. It is for those who don't want to plateau, those who would rather die before their convictions do.

I hope reading this book will convince you of something: that by surrendering yourself totally to God's purposes, He will bring you the most pleasure in this life and the next. I hope it affirms your desire for "more God"—even if you are surrounded by people who feel they have "enough God." I hope it inspires confidence if you have questioned and doubted the commitment of the American church. I want to affirm your questioning, even while assuring you there is hope.

God put me in Simi Valley, California, to lead a church of comfortable people into lives of risk and adventure. I believe He wants us to love others so much that we go to extremes to help them. I believe He wants us to be known for giving—of our time, our money, and our abilities—and to start a movement of "giving" churches. In so doing, we can alleviate the suffering in the world and change the reputation of His bride in America. Some people, even some at my church, have told me flat-out, "You're crazy." But I can't imagine devoting my life to a greater vision.

We need to stop giving people excuses not to believe in God. You've probably heard the expression "I believe in God, just not organized religion." I don't think people would say that if the church truly lived like we are called to live. The expression would change to "I can't deny what the church does, but I don't believe in their God." At least then they'd address their rejection of God rather than use the church as a scapegoat.

We are going to look at how the Bible calls us to live our lives. It is important that we not measure our spiritual health by the people around us, who are pretty much like us. To begin this journey, we'll first address our inaccurate view of God and, consequently, of ourselves.

But before we look at what is wrong and address it, we need to understand something. The core problem isn't the fact that we're lukewarm, halfhearted, or stagnant Christians. The crux of it all is why we are this way, and it is because we have an inaccurate view of God. We see Him as a benevolent Being who is satisfied when people manage to fit Him into their lives in some small way. We forget that God never had an identity crisis. He knows that He's great and deserves to be the center of our lives. Jesus came humbly as a servant, but He never begs us to give Him some small part of ourselves. He commands everything from His followers.

The first three chapters are absolutely foundational to this book. Though parts of it may not be "new" material to you, allow these sacred truths to move you to worship. I pray that your reading of the next few pages will be interrupted by spontaneous and meaningful praise to God. Allow these words to communicate old truths to your heart in a fresh way.

After the foundation has been laid in the first three chapters, the last seven chapters call us to examine ourselves. We will address life in light of the crux of who God is. We'll discover what is wrong in our churches and, ultimately, in ourselves.

Come with me on this journey. I don't promise it will be painless. Change, as we all know, is uncomfortable. It's up to you to respond to what you read. But you will have a choice: to adjust how you live daily or to stay the same.

7/1/10 — How will this impact me for
the next year, 5 years, 10 years.

↓↑  CHAPTER ONE

---

# Stop praying

What if I said, "Stop praying"? What if I told you to stop talking *at* God for a while, but instead to take a long, hard look at Him before you speak another word? Solomon warned us not to rush into God's presence with words. That's what fools do. And often, that's what we do.

We are a culture that relies on technology over community, a society in which spoken and written words are cheap, easy to come by, and excessive. Our culture says anything goes; fear of God is almost unheard of. We are slow to listen, quick to speak, and quick to become angry.

The wise man comes to God without saying a word and stands in awe of Him. It may seem a hopeless endeavor, to gaze at the invisible God. But Romans 1:20 tells us that through creation, we see His "invisible qualities" and "divine nature."

Let's begin this book by gazing at God in silence. What I want you to do right now is to go online and look at the "Awe Factor" video at www.crazylovebook.com to get a taste of the awe factor of our God. Seriously—go do it.

Speechless? Amazed? Humbled?

When I first saw those images, I *had* to worship. I didn't want to speak to or share it with anyone. I just wanted to sit quietly and admire the Creator.

It's wild to think that most of these galaxies have been discovered only in the past few years, thanks to the Hubble telescope. They've been in the universe for thousands of years without humans even knowing about them.

Why would God create more than 350,000,000,000 galaxies (and this is a conservative estimate) that generations of people never saw or even knew existed? Do you think maybe it was to make us say, "Wow, God is unfathomably big"? Or perhaps God wanted us to see these pictures so that our response would be, "Who do I think I am?"

R. C. Sproul writes, "Men are never duly touched and impressed with a conviction of their insignificance, until they have contrasted themselves with the majesty of God."[1]

↓↑

Switch gears with me for a minute and think about the detailed intricacy of the other side of creation.

Did you know that a caterpillar has 228 separate and distinct muscles in its head? That's quite a few, for a bug. The average elm tree has approximately *6 million* leaves on it. And your own heart generates enough pressure as it pumps blood throughout your body that it could squirt blood up to 30 feet. (I've never tried this, and I don't recommend it.)

Have you ever thought about how diverse and creative God is? He didn't have to make hundreds of different kinds of bananas, but He did. He didn't have to put 3,000 different species of trees within one square mile in the Amazon jungle, but He did. God didn't have to create so many kinds of laughter. Think about the different sounds of your friends' laughs—wheezes, snorts, silent, loud, obnoxious.

How about the way plants defy gravity by drawing water upward from the ground into their stems and veins? Or did you know that spiders produce three kinds of silk? When they build their webs, they create sixty feet of silk in one hour, simultaneously producing special oil on their feet that prevents them from sticking to their own web. (Most of us hate spiders, but sixty feet an hour deserves some respect!) Coral plants are so sensitive that they can die if the water temperature varies by even one or two degrees.

Did you know that when you get goose bumps, the hair in your follicles is actually helping you stay warmer by trapping body heat? Or what about the simple fact that plants take in carbon dioxide (which is harmful to us) and produce oxygen (which we need to survive)? I'm sure you knew that, but have you ever marveled at it? And these same poison-swallowing, life-giving plants came from tiny seeds that were placed in the dirt. Some were watered, some weren't; but after a few days they poked through the soil and out into the warm sunlight.

Whatever God's reasons for such diversity, creativity, and sophistication in the universe, on earth, and in our own bodies, the point of it all is His glory. God's art speaks of Himself, reflecting who He is and what He is like.

> The heavens declare the glory of God; the skies proclaim the work of his hands. Day after day they pour forth speech; night after night they display knowledge. There is no speech or language where their voice is not heard. Their voice goes out into all the earth, their words to the ends of the world.
>
> —Psalm 19:1–4

This is why we are called to worship Him. His art, His handiwork, and His creation all echo the truth that He is glorious. There is no other like Him. He is the King of Kings, the Beginning and the End, the One who was and is and is to come. I know you've heard this before, but I don't want you to miss it.

I sometimes struggle with how to properly respond to God's magnitude in a world bent on ignoring or merely tolerating Him. But know this: God will not be tolerated. He instructs us to worship and fear Him.

Go back and reread the last two paragraphs. Go to the Web site www.crazylovebook.com and watch the "Just Stop and Think" fifteen-minute video. Close this book if you need to, and meditate on the almighty One who dwells in unapproachable light, the glorious One.

↓↑

There is an epidemic of spiritual amnesia going around, and none of us is immune. No matter how many fascinating details we learn about God's creation, no matter how many pictures we see of His galaxies, and no matter how many sunsets we watch, we still forget.

Most of us know that we are supposed to love and fear God; that we are supposed to read our Bibles and pray so that we can get to know Him better; that we are supposed to worship Him with our lives. But actually living it out is challenging.

It confuses us when loving God is hard. Shouldn't it be easy to love a God so wonderful? When we love God because we feel we *should* love Him, instead of genuinely loving out of our true selves, we have forgotten who God really is. Our amnesia is flaring up again.

It may sound "un-Christian" to say that on some mornings I don't feel like loving God, or I just forget to. But I do. In our world, where hundreds of things distract us from God, we have to intentionally and consistently remind ourselves of Him.

I recently attended my high school reunion. People kept coming up to me and saying, "She's *your* wife?" They were amazed, I guess, that a woman so beautiful would marry someone like me. It happened enough times that I took a good look at a photograph of the two of us. I, too, was taken aback. It *is* astonishing that my wife chooses to be with me—and not just because she is beautiful. I was reminded of the fullness of what I have been given in my wife.

We need the same sort of reminders about God's goodness. We are programmed to focus on what we don't have, bombarded multiple times throughout the day with what we need to buy that will make us feel happier or sexier or more at peace. This dissatisfaction transfers over to our thinking about God. We forget that we already have everything we need in Him. Because we don't often think about the reality of who God is, we quickly forget that He is worthy to be worshipped and loved. We are to fear Him.

A. W. Tozer writes,

What comes into our minds when we think about God is the most important thing about us.... Worship is pure or base as the worshiper entertains high or low thoughts of God. For this reason the gravest question before the Church is always God Himself, and the most portentous fact about any man is not what he at a given time may say or do, but what he in his deep heart conceives God to be like.[2]

If the "gravest question" before us really is what God Himself is like, how do we learn to know Him?

We have seen how He is the Creator of both the magnitude of the galaxies and the complexity of caterpillars. But what is He like? What are His characteristics? What are His defining attributes? How are we to fear Him? To speak to Him? Don't check out here. We need to be reminded of this stuff. It is both basic and crucial.

**God is holy.** A lot of people say that whatever you believe about

God is fine, so long as you are sincere. But that is comparable to describing your friend in one instance as a three-hundred-pound sumo wrestler and in another as a five-foot-two, ninety-pound gymnast. No matter how sincere you are in your explanations, both descriptions of your friend simply cannot be true.

The preposterous part about our doing this to God is that He already has a name, an identity. We don't get to decide who God is. "God said to Moses, 'I am who I am'" (Ex. 3:14). We don't change that.

To say that God is holy is to say that He is set apart, distinct from us. And because of His set apart–ness, there is no way we can ever fathom all of who He is. To the Jews, saying something three times demonstrated its perfection, so to call God "Holy, Holy, Holy" is to say that He is perfectly set apart, with nothing and no one to compare Him to. *That* is what it means to be "holy."

Many Spirit-filled authors have exhausted the thesaurus in order to describe God with the glory He deserves. His perfect holiness, by definition, assures us that our words can't contain Him. Isn't it a comfort to worship a God we cannot exaggerate?

**God is eternal.** Most of us would probably agree with that statement. But have you ever seriously meditated on what it means? Each of us had a beginning; everything in existence began on a particular day, at a specific time.

Everything, that is, but God. He always has been, since before there was an earth, a universe, or even angels. God exists outside of time, and since we are within time, there is no way we will ever totally grasp that concept.

Not being able to fully understand God is frustrating, but it is ridiculous for us to think we have the right to limit God to something we are capable of comprehending. What a stunted, insignificant god *that* would be! If my mind is the size of a soda can and God is the size of all the oceans, it would be stupid for me to say He is only the small amount of water I can scoop into my little can. God is so much bigger, so far beyond our time-encased, air/food/sleep–dependent lives.

Please stop here, even if just for a moment, and glorify the eternal God: "But you, O LORD, sit enthroned forever; your renown endures through all generations…. But you remain the same, and your years will never end" (Ps. 102:12, 27).

**God is all-knowing.** Isn't this an intimidating thought?

Each of us, to some degree, fools our friends and family about who we really are. But it's impossible to do that with God. He knows each of us, deeply and specifically. He knows our thoughts before we think them, our actions before we commit them, whether we are lying down or sitting or walking around. He knows who we are and what we are about. We cannot escape Him, not even if we want to. When I grow weary of trying to be faithful to Him and want a break, it doesn't come as a surprise to God.

For David, God's knowledge led him to worship. He viewed it as wonderful and meaningful. He wrote in Psalm 139 that even in the darkness he couldn't hide from God; that while he was in his mother's womb, God was there.

Hebrews 4:13 says, "Nothing in all creation is hidden from God's sight. Everything is uncovered and laid bare before the eyes of him to whom we must give account." It is sobering to realize that this is the same God who is holy and eternal, the Maker of the billions of galaxies and thousands of tree species in the rainforest. This is the God who takes the time to know all the little details about each of us. He does not have to know us so well, but He chooses to.

**God is all-powerful.** Colossians 1:16 tells us that everything was created *for* God: "For by him all things were created: things in heaven and on earth, visible and invisible, whether thrones or powers or rulers or authorities; all things were created by him and for him."

Don't we live instead as though God is created for *us*, to do *our* bidding, to bless *us*, and to take care of *our* loved ones?

Psalm 115:3 reveals, "Our God is in heaven; he does whatever pleases him." Yet we keep on questioning Him: "Why did You make me with this body, instead of that one?" "Why are so many people dying of starvation?" "Why are there so many planets with nothing living on them?" "Why is my family so messed up?" "Why don't You make Yourself more obvious to the people who need You?"

The answer to each of these questions is simply this: because He's God. He has more of a right to ask us why so many people are starving. As much as we want God to explain himself to us, His creation, we are in no place to demand that He give an account to us.

All the peoples of the earth are regarded as nothing. He does
as he pleases with the powers of heaven and the peoples of
the earth. No one can hold back his hand or say to him:
"What have you done?"

—Daniel 4:35

Can you worship a God who isn't obligated to explain His actions to you? Could it be your arrogance that makes you think God owes you an explanation?

Do you really believe that compared to God, "all the peoples of the earth are regarded as nothing," including you?

**God is fair and just.** One definition of justice is "reward and/or penalty as deserved." If what we truly deserved were up to us, we would end up with as many different answers as people who responded. But it isn't up to us, mostly because none of us are good.

God is the only Being who is good, and the standards are set by Him. Because God hates sin, He has to punish those guilty of sin. Maybe that's not an appealing standard. But to put it bluntly, when you get your own universe, you can make your own standards. When we disagree, let's not assume it's His reasoning that needs correction.

It takes a lot for us to comprehend God's total hatred for sin. We make excuses like, "Yes, I am prideful at times, but everyone struggles with pride." However, God says in Proverbs 8:13, "I *hate* pride and arrogance." You and I are not allowed to tell Him how much He can hate it. He can hate and punish it as severely as His justice demands.

God never excuses sin. And He is always consistent with that ethic. Whenever we start to question whether God really hates sin, we have only to think of the cross, where His Son was tortured, mocked, and beaten because of sin. *Our* sin.

No question about it: God hates and must punish sin. And He is totally just and fair in doing so.

## Before the Throne

So far we have talked about things we can see with our own eyes, things we know about creation, and some of the attributes of God as revealed in the Bible. But many facets of God expand beyond our comprehension. He cannot be contained in this world, explained by our vocabulary, or grasped by our understanding.

Yet in Revelation 4 and Isaiah 6 we get two distinct glimpses of the heavenly throne room. Let me paint a bit of a word picture for you.

In Revelation, when John recounts his experience of seeing God, it's as though he's scrambling for earthly words to describe the vision he was privileged to see. He describes the One seated on the throne with two gems, "jasper and carnelian," and the area around the throne as a rainbow that looked like an emerald. God, the One on the throne, resembles radiant jewels more than flesh and blood.

This sort of poetic, artistic imagery can be difficult for those of us who don't think that way. So imagine the most stunning sunset you've ever seen. Remember the radiant colors splashed across the sky? The way you stopped to gaze at it in awe? And how the words *wow* and *beautiful* seemed so lacking? That's a small bit of what John is talking about in Revelation 4 as he attempts to articulate his vision of heaven's throne room.

John describes "flashes of lightning" and "rumblings and peals of thunder" coming from God's throne, a throne that must be unlike any other. He writes that before the throne are seven blazing torches and something like a sea of glass that looks like crystal. Using ordinary words, he does his best to describe a heavenly place and a holy God.

Most intriguing to me is how John describes those who surround the throne. First, there are the twenty-four elders dressed in white and wearing golden crowns. Next, John describes four six-winged beings with eyes all over their bodies and wings. One has the face of a lion, one of an ox, one of a man, and one of an eagle.

I try to imagine what it would be like if I actually saw one of these creatures out in the woods or down at the beach. I would probably pass out! It would be terrifying to see a being with the face of a lion and eyes "all around and within."

As if John's description isn't wild and strange enough, he then tells us what the beings are saying. The twenty-four elders cast their gold crowns before the One on the throne, fall on their faces before Him, and say, "You are worthy, our Lord and God, to receive glory and honor and power, for you created all things, and by your will they were created and have their being." At the same time, the four creatures never stop (day or night) saying, "Holy, holy, holy is the Lord God Almighty, who was, and is, and is to come!" Just imagine being in that room, surrounded by the elders chanting God's worth, and the creatures declaring God's holiness.

The prophet Isaiah also had a vision of God in His throne room, but this time it is a more direct picture: "I saw the Lord seated on a throne."

*Wow.* Isaiah saw that and lived? The Israelites hid themselves whenever God passed by their camp because they were too afraid to look at Him, even the back of Him as He moved away. They were scared they would die if they saw God.

But Isaiah looked and saw God. He writes that the bottom of God's robe filled the whole temple, and that the seraphim appeared above Him. The seraphim each had six wings, similar to the creatures John describes in Revelation. Isaiah says they called out to one another, saying, "Holy, holy, holy is the LORD Almighty; the whole earth is full of his glory!" Then the foundations shook and smoke filled the house, which is similar to John's description of flashes of lightning and peals of thunder.

Isaiah's description is less detailed than John's, but Isaiah shares more of his response to being in the throne room of God. His words reverberate in the wake of the smoky room and shaky foundation: "Woe is me.… I am ruined! For I am a man of unclean lips, and my eyes have seen the King, the LORD Almighty." And then one of the seraphim brings Isaiah a piece of burning coal that had been smoldering on the altar. The creature touches Isaiah's mouth with the hot coal and tells him that his guilt is taken away.

Both of these descriptions serve a purpose. John's helps us imagine what the throne room of God looks like, while Isaiah's reminds us what our only response to such a God should be.

May Isaiah's cry become our own. Woe is me … we are a people of unclean lips!

⇅

Perhaps you need to take a deep breath after thinking about the God who made galaxies and caterpillars, the One who sits enthroned and eternally praised by beings so fascinating that were they photographed, it would make primetime news for weeks. If you are not staggered, go to Isaiah 6 and Revelation 4 and read the accounts aloud and slowly, doing your best to imagine what the authors describe.

# you might not finish this chapter

You could die before you finish reading this chapter. I could die while you're reading it. Today. At any moment.

But it's easy to think about today as just another day. An average day where you go about life concerned with your to-do list, preoccupied by appointments, focused on family, thinking about your desires and needs.

On the average day, we live caught up in ourselves. On the average day, we don't consider God very much. On the average day, we forget that our life truly is a vapor.

But there is nothing normal about today. Just think about everything that must function properly just for you to survive. For example, your kidneys. The only people who really think about their kidneys are people whose kidneys don't work correctly. The majority of us take for granted our kidneys, liver, lungs, and other internal organs that we're dependent upon to continue living.

What about driving down the road at sixty-five miles per hour, only a few feet away from cars going the opposite direction at the same speed? Someone would only have to jerk his or her arm and you would be dead. I don't think that's morbid; I think it's reality.

It's crazy that we think today is just a normal day to do whatever we want with. To those of us who say, "Today or tomorrow we will go to this or that city, spend a year there, carry on business and make money," James writes, "Why, you do not even know what will happen tomorrow. What is your life? You are a mist that appears for a little while and then vanishes" (4:13–14).

When you think about it, that's a little disconcerting. But even after reading those verses, do you really believe you could vanish at any minute? That perhaps today you will die? Or do you instead feel somehow invincible?

Frederick Buechner writes, "Intellectually we all know that we will die, but we do not really know it in the sense that the knowledge becomes a part of us. We do not really know it in the sense of living as though it were true. On the contrary, we tend to live as though our lives would go on forever."[3]

## Justified Stress?

I had never experienced heart problems until a couple of years ago when I began to have heart palpitations. Over time they became more frequent, and this worried me.

I finally told my wife. In case something happened to me, I didn't want it to come as a complete shock. She suggested I go to the doctor, but I resisted because I'm stubborn and that's what I do.

You see, when I was honest I knew what the problem was. I was immersed in and overcome by stress. It was the Christmas season, and I had to take care of and think about a lot of things.

But on Christmas Eve the issue intensified so much that I told my wife I would go to the emergency room after the church service. During the service, however, I surrendered all of my worries and stress to God. My symptoms slowly went away, and I never went to the doctor.

I used to believe that in this world there are two kinds of people: natural worriers and naturally joyful people. I couldn't really help it that I was the worrying kind. I'm a problem solver, so I have to focus on things that need fixing. God can see that my intensity and anxiety are ministry related. I worry because I take His work seriously.

Right?

But then there's that perplexing command: "*Rejoice in the Lord always.* I will say it again: Rejoice!" (Phil. 4:4). You'll notice that it doesn't end with "… unless you're doing something extremely important." No, it's a command for all of us, and it follows with the charge, "Do not be anxious about anything" (v. 6).

That came as a pretty staggering realization. But what I realized next was even more staggering.

When I am consumed by my problems—stressed out about *my* life, *my* family, and *my* job—I actually convey the belief that I think the circumstances are more important than God's command to always rejoice. In other words, that I have a "right" to disobey God because of the magnitude of my responsibilities.

**Worry** implies that we don't quite trust that God is big enough, powerful enough, or loving enough to take care of what's happening in our lives.

**Stress** says that the things we are involved in are important enough to merit our impatience, our lack of grace toward others, or our tight grip of control.

Basically, these two behaviors communicate that it's okay to sin and not trust God because the stuff in my life is somehow exceptional. Both worry and stress reek of arrogance. They declare our tendency to forget that we've been forgiven, that our lives here are brief, that we are headed to a place where we won't be lonely, afraid, or hurt ever again, and that in the context of God's strength, our problems are small, indeed.

Why are we so quick to forget God? Who do we think we are?

I find myself relearning this lesson often. Even though I glimpse God's holiness, I am still dumb enough to forget that life is all about God and not about me at all.

It goes sort of like this....

Suppose you are an extra in an upcoming movie. You will probably scrutinize that one scene where hundreds of people are milling around, just waiting for that two-fifths of a second when you can see the back of your head. Maybe your mom and your closest friend get excited about that two-fifths of a second with you ... *maybe*. But no one else will realize it is you. Even if you tell them, they won't care.

Let's take it a step further. What if you rent out the theater on opening night and invite all your friends and family to come see the new movie about you? People will say, "You're an idiot! How could you think this movie is about you?"

Many Christians are even more delusional than the person I've been describing. So many of us think and live like the movie of life is all about us.

Now consider the movie of life....

*God* creates the world. (Were you alive then? Was *God* talking to you when He proclaimed "It is good" about all He had just made?)

Then people rebel against *God* (who, if you haven't realized it yet, is the main character in this movie), and *God* floods the earth to rid it of the mess people made of it.

Several generations later, *God* singles out a ninety-nine-year-old man called Abram and makes him the father of a nation (did you have anything to do with this?).

Later, along come Joseph and Moses and many other ordinary and inadequate people that the movie is also not about. *God* is the one who picks them and directs them and works miracles through them.

In the next scene, *God* sends judges and prophets to His nation because the people can't seem to give Him the one thing He asks of them (obedience).

And then, the climax: The Son of *God* is born among the people whom *God* still somehow loves. While in this world, the Son teaches His followers what true love looks like. Then the Son of *God* dies and is resurrected and goes back up to be with *God*.

And even though the movie isn't quite finished yet, we know what the last scene holds. It's the scene I already described in chapter 1: the throne room of *God*. Here every being worships *God* who sits on the throne, for He alone is worthy to be praised.

From start to finish, this movie is obviously about God. He is the main character. *How is it possible that we live as though it is about us?* Our scenes in the movie, our brief lives, fall somewhere between the time Jesus ascends into heaven (Acts) and when we will all worship God on His throne in heaven (Revelation).

We have only our two-fifths-of-a-second-long scene to live. I don't know about you, but I want my two-fifths of a second to be about my making much of God. First Corinthians 10:31 says, "So whether you eat or drink or whatever you do, do it all for the glory of God." That is what each of our two-fifths of a second is about.

So what does that mean for you?

Frankly, you need to get over yourself. It might sound harsh, but that's seriously what it means.

Maybe life's pretty good for you right now. God has given you this good stuff so that you can show the world a person who enjoys blessings, but who is still totally obsessed with God.

Or maybe life is tough right now, and everything feels like a struggle. God has allowed hard things in your life so you can show the world that your God is great and that knowing Him brings peace and joy, even when life is hard. Like the psalmist who wrote, "I saw the prosperity of the wicked.... Surely in vain have I kept my heart pure.... When I tried to understand all this, it was oppressive to me *till I entered the sanctuary of God*" (Ps. 73:3, 13, 16–17). It is easy to become disillusioned with the circumstances of our lives compared to others'. But in the presence of God, He gives us a deeper peace and joy that transcends it all.

To be brutally honest, it doesn't really matter what place you find yourself in right now. Your part is to bring Him glory—whether eating a sandwich on a lunch break, drinking coffee at 12:04 a.m. so you can stay awake to study, or watching your four-month-old take a nap.

The point of your life is to point to Him. Whatever you are doing,

God wants to be glorified, because this whole thing is His. It is His movie, His world, His gift.

## Thank God We Are Weak

So even though *God* has given us this life—this brief scene in His movie—we still forget we're not in control.

I was reminded of life's fragility by the birth of my fourth child and only son. All of a sudden our little girls wanted to carry their new baby brother around. My wife and I constantly told them to be careful because he's fragile. It got me wondering when he would no longer be fragile. When he's two? Eight? In junior high? College? Married? Once he has kids?

Isn't life always fragile? It is never under control. Even as I sat holding my son, I realized that I couldn't control whether he would love God.

Ultimately, I have just as little control over my own life and what will happen to me. Isn't the easiest thing at this point to start living in a guarded, safe, controlled way? To stop taking risks and to be ruled by our fears of what could happen?

Turning inward is one way to respond; the other is to acknowledge our lack of control and reach out for God's help.

If life were stable, I'd never need God's help. Since it's not, I reach out for Him regularly. I am thankful for the unknowns and that I don't have control, because it makes me run to God.

Just to put into perspective the brevity of our lives:

Throughout time, somewhere between forty-five billion and one hundred twenty-five billion people have lived on this earth.[4] That's 125,000,000,000. In about fifty years (give or take a couple of decades), no one will remember you. Everyone you know will be dead. Certainly no one will care what job you had, what car you drove, what school you attended, or what clothes you wore. This can be terrifying or reassuring, or maybe a mix of both.

## Are You Ready?

As a pastor, I'm often called upon when life "vanishes like a mist." One of the most powerful examples I've seen of this was Stan Gerlach, a successful businessman who was well known in the community. Stan was giving a eulogy at a memorial service when he decided to share the gospel. At the end of his message, Stan told the mourners, "You never know when God is going to take your life. At that moment, there's nothing you can do about it. Are you ready?" Then Stan sat down, fell over, and died. His wife and sons tried to resuscitate him, but there was nothing they could do—just as Stan had said a few minutes earlier.

I'll never forget receiving that phone call and heading over to the Gerlach house. Stan's wife, Suzy, was just arriving home. She hugged me and cried. One of her sons, John, stepped out of the car weeping. He asked me, "Did you hear the story? Did you hear? I'm so proud of him. My dad died doing what he loved doing most. He was telling people about Jesus."

I was asked to share a word with everyone gathered. There were children, grandchildren, neighbors, and friends. I opened my Bible to Matthew 10:32–33: "Whoever acknowledges me before men, I will also acknowledge him before my Father in heaven. But whoever disowns me before men, I will disown him before my Father in heaven."

I asked everyone to imagine what it must have felt like for Stan. One moment, he was at a memorial service saying to a crowd, "This is who Jesus is!" The next, he was before God hearing Jesus say, "This is who Stan Gerlach is!" One second he was confessing Jesus; a second later, Jesus was confessing him!

It happens that quickly. And it could happen to any of us. In the words of Stan Gerlach, "Are you ready?"

⇵

Brooke Bronkowski was a beautiful fourteen-year-old girl who was in love with Jesus. When she was in junior high, she started a Bible study on her campus. She spent her babysitting money on Bibles so she could give them out to her unsaved friends. Youth pastors who heard about this brought her boxes of Bibles to give away.

Brooke wrote the following essay when she was about twelve; it will give you an idea of the kind of girl she was.

# "SINCE I HAVE MY LIFE BEFORE ME"
### By Brooke Bronkowski

*I'll live my life to the fullest. I'll be happy. I'll brighten up. I will be more joyful than I have ever been. I will be kind to others. I will loosen up. I will tell others about Christ. I will go on adventures and change the world. I will be bold and not change who I really am. I will have no troubles but instead help others with their troubles.*

*You see, I'll be one of those people who live to be history makers at a young age. Oh, I'll have moments, good and bad, but I will wipe away the bad and only remember the good. In fact that's all I remember, just good moments, nothing in between, just living my life to the fullest. I'll be one of those people who go somewhere with a mission, an awesome plan, a world-changing plan, and nothing will hold me back. I'll set an example for others, I will pray for direction.*

*I have my life before me. I will give others the joy I have and God will give me more joy. I will do everything God tells me to do. I will follow the footsteps of God. I will do my best!!!*

During her freshman year in high school, Brooke was in a car accident while driving to the movies. Her life on earth ended when she was just fourteen, but her impact didn't. Nearly fifteen hundred people attended Brooke's memorial service. People from her public high school read poems she had written about her love for God. Everyone spoke of her example and her joy.

I shared the gospel and invited those who wanted to know Jesus to come up and give their lives to Him. There must have been at least two hundred students on their knees at the front of the church praying for salvation. Ushers gave a Bible to each of them. They were Bibles that Brooke had kept in her garage, hoping to give out to all of her unsaved friends. In one day, Brooke led more people to the Lord than most ever will.

In her brief fourteen years on earth, Brooke was faithful to Christ. Her short life was not wasted. The words from her essay seem prophetic: *"You see, I'll be one of those people who live to be history makers at a young age."*

We've all been shocked to hear about or watch someone we know pass on from this life. Even as you read this, faces and names are probably coming to mind. It's good to think about those people in your life, and also to think about death. As the author of Ecclesiastes wrote, "It is better to go to a house of mourning than to go to a house of feasting, for death is the destiny of every man; the living should take this to heart" (7:2). Stories of people who died after living godly lives are stories with happy endings.

Sadly, many people die while living selfishly. Their funerals are filled by individuals who stretch the truth in order to create a semblance of a meaningful life. Nobody would dare say an unkind word at the funeral; there is an unspoken obligation to come up with something nice to say about the person who died. But sometimes we secretly think the same thing: *He really wasn't that great of a person.*

The truth is, some people waste their lives. This isn't meant to bash those who are gone, but rather to warn those who are alive.

I can pretty much guarantee you that your funeral will be nice.

They all are. The fact is, at that point, you won't care. A. W. Tozer once said, "A man by his sin may waste himself, which is to waste that which on earth is most like God. This is man's greatest tragedy and God's heaviest grief."

When we face the holy God, "nice" isn't what we will be concerned with, and it definitely isn't what He will be thinking about. Any compliments you received on earth will be gone; all that will be left for you is truth. The church in Sardis had a great reputation, but it didn't matter. Jesus said to them, "I know your deeds; you have a reputation of being alive, but you are dead" (Rev. 3:1). All that matters is the reality of who we are before God.

> His work will be shown for what it is, because the Day will bring it to light. It will be revealed with fire, and the fire will test the quality of each man's work. If what he has built survives, he will receive his reward. If it is burned up, he will suffer loss; he himself will be saved, but only as one escaping through the flames.
>
> —1 Corinthians 3:13–15

Perhaps that sounds harsh, but harsh words and the loving truth often go hand in hand.

I think it's easy to hear a story like Brooke's and just move on, without acknowledging that it could just as easily be you or me or my wife or your brother whose life ends suddenly. You could be the next person in your family to die. I could be the next person at my church to die.

We have to *realize* it. We have to believe it enough that it changes how we live.

A friend of mine has a particularly wise perspective on this subject. He was asked if he weren't spending too much of his time serving and giving too much away. His gentle but honest response was, "I wonder if you'll say that after we're dead."

Friends, we need to stop living selfish lives, forgetful of our God. Our lives here are short, often unexpectedly so, and we can all stand to be reminded of it from time to time. That's why I wrote this chapter, to help us remember that in the movie of life, nothing matters except our King and God.

Don't let yourself forget. Soak it in and keep remembering that it is true. He is everything.

---

# crazy love

I was taught the song "Jesus Loves Me" as a young child: "Jesus loves me, this I know …" Even if you didn't grow up in a church, you probably know how it ends: "… for the Bible tells me so."

If you've spent any time in church, you've heard expressed, in some form or another, the idea that God loves us. I believed this for years because, as the song puts it, "the Bible tells me so." The only problem is that it was a concept I was taught, not something I implicitly knew to be true. For years I "got" God's love in my head, checked the right answer on the "what God is like" test, but didn't fully understand it with my heart.

I don't think I'm the only person who has misunderstood God's love. Most of us, to some degree, have a difficult time understanding, believing, or accepting God's absolute and unlimited love for us. The reasons we don't receive, trust, or see His love vary from one person to the next, but we all miss out because of it.

For me, it had much to do with my relationship with my own father.

## dad and DAD

The concept of being wanted by a father was foreign to me. Growing up, I felt unwanted by my dad. My mother died giving birth to me, so maybe he saw me as the cause of her death; I'm not sure.

I never carried on a meaningful conversation with my dad. In fact, the only affection I remember came when I was nine years old: He put his arm around me for about thirty seconds while we were on our way to my stepmother's funeral. Besides that, the only other physical touch I experienced were the beatings I received when I disobeyed or bothered him.

My goal in our relationship was not to annoy my father. I would walk around the house trying not to upset him.

He died when I was twelve. I cried but also felt relief.

The impact of this relationship affected me for years, and I think a lot of those emotions transferred to my relationship with God. For example, I tried hard not to annoy God with my sin or upset Him with my little problems. I had no aspiration of being wanted by God; I was just happy not to be hated or hurt by Him.

Don't get me wrong. Not everything about my dad was bad. I really do thank God for him, because he taught me discipline, respect, fear, and obedience. I also think he loved me. But I can't sugarcoat how my relationship with him negatively affected my view of God for many years.

Thankfully, my relationship with God took a major turn when I became a father myself. After my oldest daughter was born, I began to see how wrong I was in my thinking about God. For the first time I got a taste of what I believe God feels toward us. I thought about my daughter often. I prayed for her while she slept at night. I showed her picture to anyone who would look. I wanted to give her the world.

Sometimes when I come home from work, my little girl greets me by running out to the driveway and jumping into my arms before I can even get out of the car. As you can imagine, arriving home has become one of my favorite moments of the day.

My own love and desire for my kids' love is so strong that it opened my eyes to how much God desires and loves us. My daughter's expression of love for me and her desire to be with me is the most amazing thing. Nothing compares to being truly, exuberantly wanted by your children.

Through this experience, I came to understand that my desire for my children is only a faint echo of God's great love for me and for every person He made. I am just an earthly, sinful father, and I love my kids so much it hurts. How could I not trust a heavenly, perfect Father who loves me infinitely more than I will ever love my kids?

> If you, then, though you are evil, know how to give good gifts to your children, how much more will your Father in heaven give good gifts to those who ask him!
>
> —Matthew 7:11

God is more worthy of trust than anyone else, yet for so long I questioned His love and doubted His care and provision for me.

## In Love with the One I Fear

If I could pick one word to describe my feelings about God in those first years of being a Christian, it would be *fear*. Basically, any verses that describe His overwhelming greatness or His wrath were easy for me to relate to because I feared my own father. I totally connected with passages like this one:

> He sits enthroned above the circle of the earth, and its people are like grasshoppers. He stretches out the heavens like a canopy, and spreads them out like a tent to live in. He brings princes to naught and reduces the rulers of this world to nothing. No sooner are they planted, no sooner are they sown, no sooner do they take root in the ground, than he blows on them and they wither, and a whirlwind sweeps them away like chaff.
>
> —Isaiah 40:22–24

Most Christians have been taught in church or by their parents to set aside a daily time for prayer and Scripture reading. It's what we are supposed to do, and so for a long time it's what I valiantly attempted. When I didn't, I felt guilty.

Over time I realized that when we love God, we naturally run to Him—frequently and zealously. Jesus didn't command that we have a regular time with Him each day. Rather, He tells us to "love the Lord your God with all your heart and with all your soul and with all your mind." He called this the "first and greatest commandment" (Matt. 22:37–38). The results are intimate prayer and study of His Word. Our motivation changes from guilt to love.

This is how God longs for us to respond to His extravagant, unending love: not with a cursory "quiet time" plagued by guilt, but with true love expressed through our lives. Like my little girl running out to the driveway to hug me each night because she loves me.

*Fear* is no longer the word I use to describe how I feel about God. Now I use words like *reverent intimacy*. I still fear God, and I pray that I always will. The Bible emphasizes the importance of fearing God. As we talked about in chapter 1, our culture severely lacks the fear of God, and many of us are plagued with amnesia. But for a long time, I narrowly focused on His fearsomeness to the exclusion of His great and abounding love.

## Wanted

Recently, out of a desire to grow in my love for God, I decided to spend a few days alone with Him in the woods.

Before I left, a friend prayed, "God, I know how You've wanted this time with Francis …" Though I didn't say anything at the time, I secretly thought it was a heretical way to pray and that he was wrong to phrase it that way. I was going to the woods because I wanted more of God. But He's *God*; He certainly wouldn't want more of me! It seemed demeaning to think that God could long for a human being.

The more I searched the Scriptures, however, the more I realized my friend's prayer was right on, and that my reaction to his prayer indicated how much I still doubted God's love. My belief in God's love was still theoretical, not a reality I lived out or experienced.

I ended up spending four days in the woods without speaking to another human being. I had no plan or agenda; I just opened my Bible. I don't think it was coincidence that on the first day it fell open to Jeremiah 1.

After reading that passage, I meditated on it for the next four days. It spoke of God's intimate knowledge of me. I had always acknowledged His complete sovereignty over me, but verses 4 and 5 took it to another level: "The word of the LORD came to me, saying, 'Before I formed you in the womb I knew you, before you were born I set you apart; I appointed you as a prophet to the nations.'"

In other words, God knew me before He made me.

Please don't skim over this truth just because you've heard it before. Take some time to really think about it. I'll say it again: *God knew you and me before we existed.*

When I first digested this, all of my other relationships seemed trivial by comparison. God has been with me from the start—in fact, from well *before* the start.

My next thought, alone in the woods, was that He determined what Jeremiah would do before he was even born. I questioned whether that was also true of me. Maybe all of this pertained only to Jeremiah's life?

Then I remembered Ephesians 2:10, which tells us that we were created "to do good works, which God prepared in advance for us to do." That verse is meant for me and all others who have been "saved by grace through faith." My existence was not random, nor was it an accident. God knew who He was creating, and He designed me for a specific work.

God's next words to Jeremiah assured me that I need not fear failure:

"Ah, Sovereign LORD," I said, "I do not know how to speak; I am only a child."

But the LORD said to me, "Do not say, 'I am only a child.' You must go to everyone I send you to and say whatever I command you. Do not be afraid of them, for I am with you and will rescue you," declares the LORD. Then the LORD reached out his hand and touched my mouth and said to me, "Now, I have put my words in your mouth. See, today I appoint you over nations and kingdoms to uproot and tear down, to destroy and overthrow, to build and to plant."

—Jeremiah 1:6–10

When Jeremiah voices his hesitation and fear, God—the God of the galaxies—reaches out and touches his mouth. It's a gentle and affectionate gesture, something a loving parent would do. Through this illustration I realized that I don't have to worry about not meeting His expectations. God will ensure my success in accordance with His plan, not mine.

This is the God we serve, the God who knew us before He made us. The God who promises to remain with us and rescue us. The God who loves us and longs for us to love Him back.

So *why*, when we constantly offend Him and are so unlovable and unloving, does God persist in loving us?

In my childhood, doing something offensive resulted in punishment, not love. Whether we admit it or not, every one of us has offended God at some point. Jesus affirmed this when He said, "No one is good— except God alone" (Luke 18:19).

So why does God still love us, despite us? I do not have an answer to this question. But I do know that if God's mercy didn't exist, there would be no hope. No matter how good we tried to be, we would be punished because of our sins.

Many people look at their lives and weigh their sins against their good deeds. But Isaiah 64:6 says, "All our righteous acts are like filthy rags." Our good deeds can never outweigh our sins.

The literal interpretation of "filthy rags" in this verse is "menstrual garments" (think used tampons … and if you're disgusted by that idea, you get Isaiah's point). It's hard to imagine something more disgusting that we could brag about or put on display. But compared to God's perfect holiness, that's how our good deeds appear.

God's mercy is a *free*, yet costly, *gift*. It cannot be earned. Our righteous acts, just like menstrual garments, certainly don't help us deserve it. The wages of sin will always be death. But because of God's mercy, sin is paid for through the death of Jesus Christ, instead of the death of you and me.

## A Strange Inheritance

The very fact that a holy, eternal, all-knowing, all-powerful, merciful, fair, and just God loves you and me is nothing short of astonishing.

The wildest part is that Jesus doesn't *have* to love us. His being is utterly complete and perfect, apart from humanity. He doesn't need me or you. Yet He wants us, chooses us, even considers us His inheritance (Eph. 1:18). The greatest knowledge we can ever have is knowing God treasures us.

That really is amazing beyond description. The holy Creator sees you as His "glorious inheritance."

The irony is that while God doesn't need us but still wants us, we desperately need God but don't really want Him most of the time. He treasures us and anticipates our departure from this earth to be with Him—and we wonder, indifferently, how much we have to do for Him to get by.

## Do I Have a Choice?

While I was speaking to some college students recently, an interesting twist on the contrast between our unresponsiveness and God's great desire for us came up. One student asked, "Why would a loving God force me to love Him?"

It seemed like a weird question. When I asked the student to clarify what he meant, he responded that God "threatens me with hell and punishment if I don't begin a relationship with Him."

The easy retort to that statement is that God doesn't force us to love Him; it's our choice. But there was a deeper issue going on, and I wasn't sure how to answer it in the moment.

Now that I've had time to think about it, I would tell that student that if God is *truly* the greatest good on this earth, would He be loving us if He didn't draw us toward what is best for us (even if that happens to be Himself)? Doesn't His courting, luring, pushing, calling, and even "threatening" demonstrate His love? If He didn't do all of that, wouldn't we accuse Him of being unloving in the end, when all things are revealed?

If someone asked you what the greatest good on this earth is, what would you say? An epic surf session? Financial security? Health? Meaningful, trusting friendships? Intimacy with your spouse? Knowing that you belong?

*The greatest good on this earth is God.* Period. God's one goal for us is Himself.

The Good News—the best news in the world, in fact—is that you can have God Himself. Do you believe that God is the greatest thing you can experience in the whole world? Do you believe that the Good News is not merely the forgiveness of your sins, the guarantee that you won't go to hell, or the promise of life in heaven?

The best things in life are gifts from the One who steadfastly loves us. But an important question to ask ourselves is this: Are we in love with God or just His stuff?

Imagine how awful it would feel to have your child say to you, "I don't really love you or want your love, but I *would* like my allowance, please." Conversely, what a beautiful gift it is to have the one you love look you in the eye and say, "I love you. Not your beauty, your money, your family, or your car. Just *you.*"

Can you say that to God?

Our love for Him always comes out of His love for us. Do you love this God who is everything, or do you just love everything He gives you? Do you really know and believe that God loves you, individually and personally and intimately? Do you see and know Him as Abba, Father?

Watch the online videos again at www.crazylovebook.com. It will remind you who you are and of the crazy, totally undeserved love of God.

↓↑ CHAPTER FOUR

# profile of the lukewarm

*It is not scientific doubt, not atheism, not pantheism, not agnosticism,*
*that in our day and in this land is likely to quench the light of the gospel.*
*It is a proud, sensuous, selfish, luxurious, church-going,*
*hollow-hearted prosperity.*[5]

So there is an incalculable, faultless, eternal God who loves the frail
beings He made with a crazy kind of love. Even though we could die
at any moment and generally think our puny lives are pretty sweet
compared to loving Him, He persists in loving us with unending, out-
rageous love.

The only way I know to respond is like the man in one of Christ's
parables:

The kingdom of heaven is like treasure hidden in a field.
When a man found it, he hid it again, and then in his joy
went and sold all he had and bought that field.

—Matthew 13:44

In this account, the man joyfully sold all that he had so that he could
obtain the only thing that mattered. He knew that what he had stum-
bled upon—the kingdom of heaven—was more valuable than anything
he had, so he went for it with everything in him.

This kind of enthusiastic response to God's love is entirely appropriate. Yet what a contrast to our typical response at discovering the
same treasure!

In the United States, numbers impress us. We gauge the success of
an event by how many people attend or come forward. We measure
churches by how many members they boast. We are wowed by big
crowds.

Jesus questioned the authenticity of this kind of record keeping.
According to the account in Luke chapter 8, when a crowd started following Him, Jesus began speaking in parables—"*so that*" those who
weren't genuinely listening wouldn't get it.

When crowds gather today, speakers are extraconscious of communicating in a way that is accessible to everyone. Speakers don't use Jesus'
tactic to eliminate people who are not sincere seekers.

The fact is, He just wasn't interested in those who fake it.

In the parable of the sower, Jesus explained that the seed is the truth
(the Word of God). When the seed is flung onto the path, it is heard but
quickly stolen away. When the seed is tossed onto the rocks, no roots

take hold; there is an appearance of depth and growth because of the good soil, but it is only surface level. When the seed is spread among the thorns, it is received but soon suffocated by life's worries, riches, and pleasures. But when the seed is sown in good soil, it grows, takes root, and produces fruit.

My caution to you is this: *Do not assume you are good soil.*

I think most American churchgoers are the soil that chokes the seed because of all the thorns. Thorns are anything that distracts us from God. When we want God and a bunch of other stuff, then that means we have thorns in our soil. A relationship with God simply cannot grow when money, sins, activities, favorite sports teams, addictions, or commitments are piled on top of it.

Most of us have too much in our lives. As David Goetz writes, "Too much of the good life ends up being toxic, deforming us spiritually."[6] A lot of things are good by themselves, but all of it together keeps us from living healthy, fruitful lives for God.

I will say it again: *Do not assume you are good soil.*

Has your relationship with God actually changed the way you live? Do you see evidence of God's kingdom in your life? Or are you choking it out slowly by spending too much time, energy, money, and thought on the things of this world?

Are you satisfied being "godly enough" to get yourself to heaven, or to look good in comparison to others? Or can you say with Paul that you "want to know Christ and the power of his resurrection and the fellowship of sharing in his sufferings, becoming like him in his death" (Phil. 3:10)?

For a long time this verse had just too much Jesus for me. In my opinion, the verse should have ended after the word *resurrection*, so I could have an appealing, popular Jesus who didn't suffer. The feedback I received from other Christians reassured me that this was a fine perspective, and it gave me little reason to strive to know Christ more deeply. I was told I was good enough, "godly enough."

But this went against everything I was reading in the Bible, so I eventually rejected what the majority said and began to compare all aspects of my life to Scripture. I quickly found that the American church is a difficult place to fit in if you want to live out New Testament Christianity. The goals of American Christianity are often a nice marriage, children who don't swear, and good church attendance. Taking the words of Christ literally and seriously is rarely considered. That's for the "radicals" who are "unbalanced" and who go "overboard." Most of us want a balanced life that we can control, that is safe, and that does not involve suffering.

Would you describe yourself as totally in love with Jesus Christ? Or do the words *halfhearted*, *lukewarm*, and *partially committed* fit better?

The Bible says to test ourselves, so in the next few pages, I am going to offer you a description of what halfhearted, distracted, partially committed, lukewarm people can look like. As you read these examples, I encourage you to take a searching, honest look at your life. Not who you want to be one of these days, but who you are now and how you are living today.

LUKEWARM PEOPLE attend church fairly regularly. It is what is expected of them, what they believe "good Christians" do, so they go.

"The Lord says: 'These people come near to me with

their mouth and honor me with their lips, but their hearts are far from me. Their worship of me is made up only of rules taught by men'" (Isa. 29:13).

LUKEWARM PEOPLE give money to charity and to the church … as long as it doesn't impinge on their standard of living. If they have a little extra and it is easy and safe to give, they do so. After all, God loves a cheerful giver, right?

"King David replied to Araunah, 'No, I insist on paying the full price. I will not take for the LORD what is yours, or sacrifice a burnt offering that costs me nothing'" (1 Chron. 21:24).

"As he looked up, Jesus saw the rich putting their gifts into the temple treasury. He also saw a poor widow put in two very small copper coins. 'I tell you the truth,' he said, 'this poor widow has put in more than all the others. All these people gave their gifts out of their wealth; but she out of her poverty put in all she had to live on'" (Luke 21:1–4).

LUKEWARM PEOPLE tend to choose what is popular over what is right when they are in conflict. They desire to fit in both at church and outside of church; they care more about what people think of their actions (like church attendance and giving) than what God thinks of their hearts and lives.

"Woe to you when all men speak well of you, for that is how their fathers treated the false prophets" (Luke 6:26).

"I know your deeds; you have a reputation of being alive, but you are dead" (Rev. 3:1).

"Everything they do is done for men to see: They make their phylacteries wide and the tassels on their garments long; they love the place of honor at banquets and the most important seats in the synagogues; they love to be greeted in the marketplaces and to have men call them 'Rabbi'" (Matt. 23:5–7).

LUKEWARM PEOPLE don't really want to be saved from their sin; they want only to be saved from the penalty of their sin. They don't genuinely hate sin and aren't truly sorry for it; they're merely sorry because God is going to punish them. Lukewarm people don't really believe that this new life Jesus offers is better than the old sinful one.

"I have come that they may have life, and have it to the full" (John 10:10).

"What shall we say, then? Shall we go on sinning so that grace may increase? By no means! We died to sin; how can we live in it any longer?" (Rom. 6:1–2).

LUKEWARM PEOPLE are moved by stories about people who

do radical things for Christ, yet they do not act. They assume such action is for "extreme" Christians, not average ones. Lukewarm people call "radical" what Jesus expected of all His followers.

"Do not merely listen to the word, and so deceive yourselves. Do what it says" (James 1:22).

"Anyone, then, who knows the good he ought to do and doesn't do it, sins" (James 4:17).

"What do you think? There was a man who had two sons. He went to the first and said, 'Son, go and work today in the vineyard.' 'I will not,' he answered, but later he changed his mind and went. Then the father went to the other son and said the same thing. He answered, 'I will, sir,' but he did not go. Which of the two did what his father wanted? 'The first,' they answered" (Matt. 21:28–31).

LUKEWARM PEOPLE rarely share their faith with their neighbors, coworkers, or friends. They do not want to be rejected, nor do they want to make people uncomfortable by talking about private issues like religion.

"Whoever acknowledges me before men, I will also acknowledge him before my Father in heaven. But whoever disowns me before men, I will disown him before my Father in heaven" (Matt. 10:32–33).

LUKEWARM PEOPLE gauge their morality or "goodness" by comparing themselves to the secular world. They feel satisfied that while they aren't as hard-core for Jesus as so-and-so, they are nowhere as horrible as the guy down the street.

"The Pharisee stood up and prayed about himself: 'God, I thank you that I am not like other men—robbers, evildoers, adulterers—or even like this tax collector. I fast twice a week and give a tenth of all I get'" (Luke 18:11–12).

LUKEWARM PEOPLE say they love Jesus, and He is, indeed, a part of their lives. But only a part. They give Him a section of their time, their money, and their thoughts, but He isn't allowed to control their lives.

"As they were walking along the road, a man said to him, 'I will follow you wherever you go.' Jesus replied, 'Foxes have holes and birds of the air have nests, but the Son of Man has no place to lay his head.' He said to another man, 'Follow me.' But the man replied, 'Lord, first let me go and bury my father.' Jesus said to him, 'Let the dead bury their own dead, but you go and proclaim the kingdom of God.' Still another said, 'I will follow you, Lord; but first let me go back and say good-by to my family.' Jesus replied, 'No one who puts his hand to the plow and looks back is fit for service in the kingdom of God'" (Luke 9:57–62).

LUKEWARM PEOPLE love God, but they do not love Him with all their heart, soul, and strength. They would be quick to assure you that they try to love God that much, but that sort of total devotion isn't really possible for the average person; it's only for pastors and missionaries and radicals.

"Jesus replied: 'Love the Lord your God with all your heart and with all your soul and with all your mind.' This is the first and greatest commandment" (Matt. 22:37–38).

LUKEWARM PEOPLE love others but do not seek to love others as much as they love themselves. Their love of others is typically focused on those who love them in return, like family, friends, and other people they know and connect with. There is little love left over for those who cannot love them back, much less for those who intentionally slight them, whose kids are better athletes than theirs, or with whom conversations are awkward or uncomfortable. Their love is highly conditional and very selective, and generally comes with strings attached.

"You have heard that it was said, 'Love your neighbor and hate your enemy.' But I tell you: Love your enemies and pray for those who persecute you, that you may be sons of your Father in heaven. He causes his sun to rise on the evil and the good, and sends rain on the righteous and the unrighteous. If you love those who love you, what reward will you get? Are not even the tax collectors doing that? And if you greet only your brothers, what are you doing more than others? Do not even pagans do that?" (Matt. 5:43–47).

"Then Jesus said to his host, 'When you give a luncheon or dinner, do not invite your friends, your brothers or relatives, or your rich neighbors; if you do, they may invite you back and so you will be repaid. But when you give a banquet, invite the poor, the crippled, the lame, the blind, and you will be blessed. Although they cannot repay you, you will be repaid at the resurrection of the righteous'" (Luke 14:12–14).

LUKEWARM PEOPLE will serve God and others, but there are limits to how far they will go or how much time, money, and energy they are willing to give.

"'All these [commandments] I have kept since I was a boy,' he said. When Jesus heard this, he said to him, 'You still lack one thing. Sell everything you have and give to the poor, and you will have treasure in heaven. Then come, follow me.' When he heard this, he became very sad, because he was a man of great wealth. Jesus looked at him and said, 'How hard it is for the rich to enter the kingdom of God! Indeed, it is easier for a camel to go through the eye of a needle than for a rich man to enter the kingdom of God'" (Luke 18:21–25).

LUKEWARM PEOPLE think about life on earth much more often than eternity in heaven. Daily life is mostly focused on today's to-do list, this week's schedule, and next month's vacation. Rarely, if ever, do they intently consider the life to come. Regarding this, C. S. Lewis writes, "If you read history you will find that the Christians who did most for the present world were precisely those who thought most of the next. It is since Christians have largely ceased to think of the other world that they have become so ineffective in this."

"For, as I have often told you before and now say again even with tears, many live as enemies of the cross of Christ. Their destiny is destruction, their god is their stomach, and their glory is in their shame. Their mind is on earthly things. But our citizenship is in heaven. And we eagerly await a Savior from there, the Lord Jesus Christ" (Phil. 3:18–20).

"Set your minds on things above, not on earthly things" (Col. 3:2).

LUKEWARM PEOPLE are thankful for their luxuries and comforts, and rarely consider trying to give as much as possible to the poor. They are quick to point out, "Jesus never said money is the root of all evil, only that the *love* of money is." Untold numbers of lukewarm people feel "called" to minister to the rich; very few feel "called" to minister to the poor.

"Come, you who are blessed by my Father; take your inheritance, the kingdom prepared for you since the creation of the world.… I tell you the truth, whatever you did for one of the least of these brothers of mine, you did for me" (Matt. 25:34, 40).

"Is not this the kind of fasting I have chosen: to loose the chains of injustice and untie the cords of the yoke, to set the oppressed free and break every yoke? Is it not to share your food with the hungry and to provide the poor wanderer with shelter—when you see the naked, to clothe him, and not to turn away from your own flesh and blood?" (Isa. 58:6–7).

LUKEWARM PEOPLE do whatever is necessary to keep themselves from feeling too guilty. They want to do the bare minimum, to be "good enough" without it requiring too much of them.

They ask, "How far can I go before it's considered a sin?" instead of "How can I keep myself pure as a temple of the Holy Spirit?"

They ask, "How much do I have to give?" instead of "How much can I give?"

They ask, "How much time should I spend praying and reading my Bible?" instead of "I wish I didn't have to go to work, so I could sit here and read longer!"

"But who am I, and who are my people, that we should be able to give as generously as this? Everything comes from you, and we have given you only what comes from your hand" (1 Chron. 29:14).

"The kingdom of heaven is like treasure hidden in a field. When a man found it, he hid it again, and then in his joy went and sold all he had and bought that field. Again, the kingdom of heaven is like a merchant looking for fine pearls. When he found one of great value, he went away and sold everything he had and bought it" (Matt. 13:44–46).

LUKEWARM PEOPLE are continually concerned with playing it safe; they are slaves to the god of control. This focus on safe living keeps them from sacrificing and risking for God.

"Command those who are rich in this present world not to be arrogant nor to put their hope in wealth, which is so uncertain, but to put their hope in God, who richly provides us with everything for our enjoyment. Command them to do good, to be rich in good deeds, and to be generous and willing to share" (1 Tim. 6:17–18).

"Do not be afraid of those who kill the body but cannot kill the soul. Rather, be afraid of the One who can destroy both soul and body in hell" (Matt. 10:28).

LUKEWARM PEOPLE feel secure because they attend church, made a profession of faith at age twelve, were baptized, come from a Christian family, vote Republican, or live in America. Just as the prophets in the Old Testament warned Israel that they were not safe just because they lived in the land of Israel, so we are not safe just because we wear the label *Christian* or because some people persist in calling us a "Christian nation."

"Not everyone who says to me, 'Lord, Lord,' will enter the kingdom of heaven, but only he who does the will of my Father who is in heaven" (Matt. 7:21).

"Woe to you who are complacent in Zion, and to you who feel secure on Mount Samaria, you notable men of the foremost nation" (Amos 6:1).

LUKEWARM PEOPLE do not live by faith; their lives are structured so they never have to. They don't have to trust God if something unexpected happens—they have their savings account. They don't need God to help them—they have their retirement plan in place. They don't genuinely seek out what life God would have them live—they have life figured and mapped out. They don't depend on God on a daily basis—their refrigerators are full and, for the most part, they are in good health. The truth is, their lives wouldn't look much different if they suddenly stopped believing in God.

"And he told them this parable: The ground of a certain rich man produced a good crop. He thought to himself, 'What shall I do? I have no place to store my crops.' Then he said, 'This is what I'll do. I will tear down my barns and build bigger ones, and there I will store all my grain and my goods. And I'll say to myself, 'You have plenty of good things laid up for many years. Take life easy; eat, drink and be merry.' But God said to him, 'You fool! This very night your life will be demanded from you. Then who will get what you have prepared for yourself?' This is how it will be with anyone who stores up things for himself but is not rich toward God" (Luke 12:16–21; see also Hebrews 11).

LUKEWARM PEOPLE probably drink and swear less than average, but besides that, they really aren't very different from your typical unbeliever. They equate their partially sanitized lives with holiness, but they couldn't be more wrong.

"Woe to you, teachers of the law and Pharisees, you hypocrites! You clean the outside of the cup and dish, but inside they are full of greed and self-indulgence. Blind Pharisee! First clean the inside of the cup and dish, and then the outside also will be clean. Woe to you, teachers of the law and Pharisees, you hypocrites! You are like whitewashed tombs, which look beautiful on the outside but on the inside are full of dead men's bones and everything unclean. In the same way, on the outside you appear to people as righteous but on the inside you are full of hypocrisy and wickedness" (Matt. 23:25–28).

This profile of the lukewarm is not an all-inclusive definition of what it means to be a Christian, nor is it intended to be used as ammunition to judge your fellow believers' salvation. Instead, as 2 Corinthians 13:5 says, it is a call to "examine yourselves, to see whether you are in the faith; test yourselves."

We are *all* messed-up human beings, and no one is totally immune to the behaviors described in the previous examples. However, there is a difference between a life that is characterized by these sorts of mentalities and habits and a life that is in the process of being radically transformed. We'll get to the transformation later, but now is the time to take a serious self-inventory.

When I was in high school, I seriously considered joining the Marines; this was when they first came out with commercials for "the few, the proud, the Marines." What turned me off was that in those advertisements, everyone was always running. Always. And I *hate* running.

But you know what? I didn't bother to ask if they would modify the rules for me so I could run less, and maybe also do fewer push-ups. That would've been pointless and stupid, and I knew it. Everyone knows that if you sign up for the Marines, you have to do whatever they tell you. They own you.

Somehow this realization does not cross over to our thinking about the Christian life. Jesus didn't say that if you wanted to follow Him you could do it in a lukewarm manner. He said, "Take up your cross and follow me." He also said,

Suppose a king is about to go to war against another king. Will he not first sit down and consider whether he is able with ten thousand men to oppose the one coming against him with twenty thousand? If he is not able, he will send a delegation while the other is still a long way off and will ask for terms of peace. In the same way, any of you who does not give up *everything* he has cannot be my disciple.

—Luke 14:31–33

Jesus asks for everything. But we try to give Him less. Jesus said,

Salt is good, but if it loses its saltiness, how can it be made salty again? It is fit neither for the soil nor for the manure pile; it is thrown out.

—Luke 14:34–35

Jesus isn't just making a cute little analogy here. He is addressing those who aren't willing to give everything, who won't follow Him all the way. He is saying that lukewarm, halfhearted following is useless, that it sickens our souls. He is saying that this kind of salt is not even fit "for the manure pile."

Wow. How would you like to hear the Son of God say, "You would ruin manure"?

When salt is salty, it helps manure become good fertilizer … but lukewarm and uncommitted faith is completely useless. It can't even benefit manure.

# serving leftovers to a holy God

Of all the chapters in this book, this one was the hardest for me to write. I do not wish for my words to come across as controversial or difficult to swallow. But I had to write this chapter, because I believe what I'm about to talk about is important. And true.

In the last chapter we discussed various inappropriate responses to God's love. Now we are going to look at scriptural examples of poor responses to God's gift of love. Before you discount or ignore what I am about to say, read these passages objectively, without preconceived opinions staunchly in place.

My examination of lukewarm Christians in chapter 4 was by no means exhaustive. However, it did serve as a call to examine your heart in light of the points I listed. As I see it, a lukewarm Christian is an oxymoron; there's no such thing. To put it plainly, churchgoers who are "lukewarm" are not Christians. We will not see them in heaven.

In Revelation 3:15–18, Jesus says,

> I know your deeds, that you are neither cold nor hot. I wish you were either one or the other! So, because you are luke-warm—neither hot nor cold—I am about to spit you out of my mouth. You say, "I am rich; I have acquired wealth and do not need a thing." But you do not realize that you are wretched, pitiful, poor, blind and naked. I counsel you to buy from me gold refined in the fire, so you can become rich; and white clothes to wear, so you can cover your shameful nakedness; and salve to put on your eyes, so you can see.

This passage is where our modern understanding of *lukewarm* comes from. Jesus is saying to the church that because they are lukewarm, He is going to spit them out of His mouth.

There is no gentle rendering of the word *spit* in Greek. This is the only time it is used in the New Testament, and it connotes gagging, hurling, retching. Many people read this passage and assume Jesus is speaking to saved people. Why?

When you read this passage, do you naturally conclude that to be "spit" out of Jesus' mouth means you're a part of His kingdom? When you read the words "wretched, pitiful, poor, blind, and naked," do you think that He's describing saints? When He counsels them to "buy white clothes to wear" in order to cover their "shameful nakedness," does it sound like advice for those already saved?

I thought people who were saved were already made white and clothed by Christ's blood.

In an earlier draft of this chapter, I quoted several commentators who agreed with my point of view. But we all know that you can find quotes to support any view you want to take. You can even tweak word studies to help you in your effort. I'm not against scholarship, but I do believe there are times when we come to more accurate conclusions through simple reading.

And so I've spent the past few days reading the Gospels. Rather than examining a verse and dissecting it, I chose to peruse one gospel in each sitting. Furthermore, I attempted to do so from the perspective of a twelve-year-old who knew nothing about Jesus. I wanted to rediscover what reasonable conclusions a person would come to while objectively reading the Gospels for the first time. In other words, I read the Bible as if I'd never read it before.

My conclusion? Jesus' call to commitment is clear: He wants all or nothing. The thought of a person calling himself a "Christian" without being a devoted follower of Christ is absurd.

But please don't take my word for it. Read it yourself.

For years I struggled with the parable of the soils. I wanted to know if the person representing the rocky soil is saved, even though he has no root. I then wondered about the thorny soil: Is this person saved since he does have root?

I doubt if people even considered these questions back in Jesus' day! Is this idea of the non-fruit-bearing Christian something that we have concocted in order to make Christianity "easier"? So we can follow our own course while still calling ourselves followers of Christ? So we can join the Marines, so to speak, without having to do all the work?

Jesus' intention in this parable was to compare the only good soil to the ones that were not legitimate alternatives. To Him, there was one option for a true believer.

Let's face it. We're willing to make changes in our lives only if we think it affects our salvation. This is why I have so many people ask me questions like, Can I divorce my wife and still go to heaven? Do I have to be baptized to be saved? Am I a Christian even though I'm having sex with my girlfriend? If I commit suicide, can I still go to heaven? If I'm ashamed to talk about Christ, is He really going to deny knowing me?

To me, these questions are tragic because they reveal much about the state of our hearts. They demonstrate that our concern is more about going to heaven than loving the King. Jesus said, "If you love me, you will obey what I command" (John 14:15). And our question quickly becomes even more unthinkable: *Can I go to heaven without truly and faithfully loving Jesus?*

I don't see anywhere in Scripture how the answer to that question could be yes.

James 2:19 says, "You believe there is one God. Good! Even the demons believe that—and shudder." God doesn't just want us to have good theology; He wants us to know and love Him. First John 2:3–4 tells us, "We know that we have come to know him if we obey his commands. The man who says, 'I know him,' but does not do what he commands is a liar, and the truth is not in him."

Call me crazy, but I think those verses mean that the person who claims to know God but doesn't obey His commands is a liar and that the truth really isn't in him.

In Matthew 16:24–25, Jesus says, "If anyone would come after me, he must deny himself and take up his cross and follow me. For whoever wants to save his life will lose it, but whoever loses his life for me will find it." And in Luke 14:33, He says, "Any of you who does not give up everything he has cannot be my disciple."

Some people claim that we can be Christians without necessarily becoming disciples. I wonder, then, why the last thing Jesus told us was to go into the world, making *disciples* of all nations, teaching them to *obey all* that He commanded? You'll notice that He *didn't* add, "But hey, if that's too much to ask, tell them to just become Christians—you know, the people who get to go to heaven without having to commit to anything."

Pray. Then read the Gospels for yourself. Put this book down and pick up your Bible. My prayer for you is that you'll understand the Scriptures not as I see them, but as God intends them.

↓↑

I do not want true believers to doubt their salvation as they read this book. In the midst of our failed attempts at loving Jesus, His *grace* covers us.

Each of us has lukewarm elements and practices in our life; therein lies the senseless, extravagant grace of it all. The Scriptures demonstrate clearly that there is room for our failure and sin in our pursuit of God.

His mercies *are* new every morning (Lamentations 3). His grace *is* sufficient (2 Corinthians 12:9). I'm *not* saying that when you mess up, it means you were never really a genuine Christian in the first place. If that were true, no one could follow Christ.

The distinction is perfection (which none will attain on this earth) and a posture of obedience and surrender, where a person perpetually moves toward Christ. To call someone a Christian simply because he does some Christian-y things is giving false comfort to the unsaved. But to declare anyone who sins "unsaved" is to deny the reality and truth of God's grace.

From other references in Scripture (Colossians 2:1; 4:13, 15–16), the church at Laodicea appears to have been a healthy and legitimate church. But something happened. By the time Revelation was written, about twenty-five years after the letter to the Colossians, the Laodiceans' hearts apparently didn't belong to God—despite the fact that they were still active as a church. Their church was prospering, and they didn't seem to be experiencing any persecution.

They were comfortable and proud. Sounds familiar, doesn't it?

## Poor Rich People

Ronnie, a blind boy who lives in eastern Uganda, is unique not because of his circumstances or the fact that he is blind, but because of his love for Jesus. If you were to meet Ronnie, one of the first things you would hear him say is, "I love Jesus so much, and I sing praises to Him every day!"

One of Ronnie's closest friends is a girl who is deaf. What stands out about these two isn't that they are handicapped or very poor, but that they are totally content and obviously in love with Jesus. They possess very little of what "counts" in our society, yet they have what matters most. They came to God in their great need, and they have found true joy.

Because we don't usually have to depend on God for food, money to buy our next meal, or shelter, we don't feel needy. In fact, we generally think of ourselves as fairly independent and capable. Even if we aren't rich, we are "doing just fine."

If one hundred people represented the world's population, fifty-three of those would live on less than $2 a day. Do you realize that if you make $4,000 a month, you automatically make *one hundred times* more than the average person on this planet? Simply by purchasing this book, you spent what a majority of people in the world will make in a week's time.

Which is more messed up—that we have so much compared to everyone else, or that we don't think we're rich? That on any given day we might flippantly call ourselves "broke" or "poor"? We are neither of those things. We are rich. Filthy rich.

Robert Murray M'Cheyne was a Scottish pastor who died at the age of twenty-nine. Although he lived in the early part of the nineteenth century, his words are astoundingly appropriate for today:

> I am concerned for the poor but more for you. I know not what Christ will say to you in the great day…. I fear there are many hearing me who may know well that they are not Christians because they do not love to give. To give largely and liberally, not grudgingly at all, requires a new heart; an old heart would rather part with its life-blood than its

money. Oh my friends! Enjoy your money; make the most of it; give none away; enjoy it quickly for I can tell you, you will be beggars throughout eternity.[7]

The reality is that, whether we acknowledge our wealth or not, being rich is a serious disadvantage spiritually. As William Wilberforce once said, "Prosperity hardens the heart."

When talking to a wealthy person who wanted to go to heaven (and doesn't that describe most of us?), Jesus said, "'Sell everything you have and give to the poor, and you will have treasure in heaven. Then come, follow me.' When he [the rich man] heard this, he became very sad, because he was a man of great wealth. Jesus looked at him and said, 'How *hard* it is for the rich to enter the kingdom of God!'" (Luke 18:22–24). He says it's as hard as a camel to go through the eye of a needle—in other words, impossible. *But then* Jesus offers hopeful words: "What is impossible with man is possible with God" (v. 27).

In the very next chapter, as Jesus enters Jericho, we see exactly how the impossible becomes possible with God. There, the wealthy tax collector Zacchaeus gives half of his money to the poor and pays everyone back four times what he has defrauded them. And Jesus declares, "Today salvation has come to this house" (Luke 19:9).

The impossible happened that day—a rich man received salvation!

## Offering Leftovers

God wants our best, deserves our best, and demands our best. From the beginning of time, He has been clear that some offerings are acceptable to Him and others are not. Just ask Cain, upon whose offering God "did not look with favor" (Gen. 4:5).

For years I gave God leftovers and felt no shame. I simply took my eyes off Scripture and instead compared myself to others. The bones I threw at God had more meat on them than the bones others threw, so I figured I was doing fine.

It's easy to fill ourselves up with other things and then give God whatever is left. Hosea 13:6 says, "When I fed them, they were satisfied; when they were satisfied, they became proud; then they forgot me." God gets a scrap or two only because we feel guilty for giving Him nothing. A mumbled three-minute prayer at the end of the day, when we are already half asleep. Two crumpled-up dollar bills thrown as an afterthought into the church's fund for the poor. Fetch, God!

> "But when you present the blind for sacrifice, is it not evil? And when you present the lame and sick, is it not evil? Why not offer it to your governor? Would he be pleased with you? Or would he receive you kindly?" says the LORD.
>
> —Malachi 1:8 NASB

The priests of Malachi's day thought their sacrifices were sufficient. They had spotless animals but chose to keep those for themselves and give their less desirable animals to God. They assumed God was pleased because they had sacrificed *something*.

God described this practice as *evil*.

Leftovers are not merely inadequate; from God's point of view (and lest we forget, His is the only one who matters), they're *evil*. Let's stop calling it "a busy schedule" or "bills" or "forgetfulness." It's called *evil*.

God is holy. In heaven exists a Being who decides whether or not I take another breath. This holy God deserves excellence, the very best I have. "But something is better than nothing!" some protest. Really, is it? Does *anyone* enjoy token praise? I sure don't. I'd rather you not say anything than compliment me out of obligation or guilt. Why would we think God is any different?

Two verses further on in Malachi, God says, "Oh that there were one among you who would shut the gates, that you might not uselessly kindle fire on My altar! I am not pleased with you, … nor will I accept an offering from you" (NASB). God wanted the temple gates shut. The weak sacrifices of the laid-back priests were an insult to Him. He was saying that no worship is better than apathetic worship. I wonder how many church doors God wants to shut today.

Jesus' instruction to the people of the church at Laodicea was to buy from Him the things that really matter, the things they didn't even realize they needed. They were wealthy, but Jesus asks them to exchange their wealth for His gold that is refined through fire; they had clothing, but Jesus counsels them to buy clothes that were truly white and would cover their nakedness; they did not desire anything, but Jesus says they needed salve for their eyes that would cure their blindness. He asks them to give up what they thought was so necessary and valuable, in exchange for what really matters.

Mark Buchanan writes, "Physical sickness we usually defy. Soul sickness we often resign ourselves to."[8] The people in Laodicea did not realize or acknowledge that their souls were sick, that they were desperately in need of what Christ offered. As Tim Kizziar said, "Our greatest fear as individuals and as a church should not be of failure but of succeeding at things in life that don't really matter."

Recently I saw a bag of potato chips with a bold declaration splashed across the front: "Zero grams of trans fat." I was glad to know that I wouldn't be consuming any trans fat, which research has shown is detrimental to my health. But then I flipped the bag over and read the ingredients list, which included things like "yellow #6" and other artificial colors, and partially hydrogenated oil (which is trans fat, just a small enough amount that they can legally call it "0 grams"). I thought it was incredibly ironic that these chips were being advertised in a way that makes me think they are not harmful yet were really full of empty calories, weird chemicals, and, ironically, trans fat.

It struck me that many Christians flash around their "no trans fat" label, trying to convince everyone they are healthy and good. Yet they have no substantive or healthful elements to their faith. It's like the Laodiceans, who thought they had everything until Christ told them they were poor and wretched. They were all about declaring, "Look, we have no trans fat. We are wealthy, or we have good families, or we go to church every week." Obviously, it's not what you advertise that counts; it's what you are really made of.

God's definition of what matters is pretty straightforward. He measures our lives by how we love. In our culture, even if a pastor doesn't actually love people, he can still be considered successful as long as he is a gifted speaker, makes his congregation laugh, or prays for "all those poor, suffering people in the world" every Sunday.

But Paul writes that even if "I have all faith, so as to remove mountains, but have not love, I am nothing. If I give away all I have, and if

I deliver up my body to be burned, but have not love, I gain nothing"
(1 Cor. 13:2–3 ESV). Wow. Those are strong and unmistakable words.
According to God, we are here to love. Not much else really matters.

So God assesses our lives based on how we love. But the word *love*
is so overused and worn out. What does God mean by love? He tells us,

> Love is patient and kind; love does not envy or boast; it is
> not arrogant or rude. It does not insist on its own way; it
> is not irritable or resentful; it does not rejoice at wrongdo-
> ing, but rejoices with the truth. Love bears all things,
> believes all things, hopes all things, endures all things. Love
> never ends…. faith, hope, and love abide, these three; but
> the greatest of these is love.
>
> —1 Corinthians 13:4–8, 13 ESV

But even those words have grown tired and overly familiar, haven't
they?

I was challenged to do a little exercise with these verses, one that was
profoundly convicting. Take the phrase *Love is patient* and substitute
your name for the word *love*. (For me, "Francis is patient….") Do it for
every phrase in the passage.

By the end, don't you feel like a liar? If I am meant to represent what
love is, then I often fail to love people well.

Following Christ isn't something that can be done halfheartedly or
on the side. It is not a label we can display when it is useful. It must be
central to everything we do and are.

If life is a river, then pursuing Christ requires swimming upstream. When we stop swimming, or actively following Him, we automatically begin to be swept downstream.

Or, to use another metaphor more familiar to city people, we are on a never-ending downward escalator. In order to grow, we have to turn around and sprint up the escalator, putting up with perturbed looks from everyone else who is gradually moving downward.

I believe that much of the American churchgoing population, while not specifically swimming downstream, is slowly floating away from Christ. It isn't a conscious choice, but it is nonetheless happening because little in their lives propels them toward Christ.

Perhaps it sounds as though I believe you have to work your way to Jesus. I don't. I fully believe that we are saved by grace, through faith, by the gift of God, and that true faith manifests itself through our actions. As James writes, "Faith by itself, if it is not accompanied by action, is dead" (2:17). The lives of many people who call themselves "Christians" in America lack manifestations of a vital and active faith.

And this, to be perfectly honest, frightens me. It keeps me up at night. It causes me to pray desperately and fervently for my congregation, for the groups of people I speak to, and for the church as a whole.

Henri Nouwen writes about this in his book *With Open Hands*: "It is hard to bear with people who stand still along the way, lose heart, and seek their happiness in little pleasures which they cling to.... You feel sad about all that self-indulgence and self-satisfaction, for you know with an indestructible certainty that something greater is coming ..."[9] Or, as Luke 9:25 says, "What good is it for a man to gain the whole world, and yet lose or forfeit his very self?"

How many of us would really leave our families, our jobs, our education, our friends, our connections, our familiar surroundings, and our homes if Jesus asked us to? If He just showed up and said, "Follow me"? No explanation. No directions.

You could follow Him straight up a hill to be crucified. Maybe He would lead you to another country, and you would never see your family again. Or perhaps you would stay put, but He would ask you to spend your time helping people who will never love you back and never show gratitude for what you gave up.

Consider this carefully—have you ever done so? Or was your decision to follow Christ flippant, based solely on feelings and emotion, made without counting the cost?

What scares me most are the people who are lukewarm and just don't care. I think that if I did a poll of the readers of this book, many of you would say, "Yeah, I am definitely lukewarm at times, but I'm not really at a place to give more to God." Many of us believe we have as much of God as we want right now, a reasonable portion of God among all the other things in our lives. Most of our thoughts are centered on the money we want to make, the school we want to attend, the body we aspire to have, the spouse we want to marry, the kind of person we want to become…. But the fact is that *nothing* should concern us more than our relationship with God; it's about eternity, and nothing compares with that. God is not someone who can be tacked on to our lives.

Remember the visions from John and Isaiah of the throne room of God? Remember the pictures of the galaxies and how tiny we are in comparison? Remember the diversity of God, seen in the thousands of species of trees in the rainforest? We say to the Creator of all this magnitude and majesty, "Well, I'm not sure You are worth it…. You see, I really like my car, or my little sin habit, or my money, and I'm really not sure I want to give them up, even if it means I get You."

When we put it plainly like this—as a direct choice between God and our stuff—most of us hope we would choose God. But we need to realize that how we spend our time, what our money goes toward, and where we will invest our energy is equivalent to choosing God or rejecting Him. How could we think for even a second that something on this puny little earth compares to the Creator and Sustainer and Savior of it all?

We disgust God when we weigh and compare Him against the things of this world. It makes Him sick when we actually decide those things are better for us than God Himself. We believe we don't need anything Jesus offers, but we fail to realize that slowly, almost imperceptibly, we are drifting downstream. And in the process we are becoming blind, being stripped naked, and turning into impoverished wretches.

No wonder Jesus says He will spit lukewarm people out of His mouth!

Hear me clearly in this, because it is vital—in fact, there is nothing more important or eternal: *Are you willing to say to God that He can have whatever He wants? Do you believe that wholehearted commitment to Him is more important than any other thing or person in your life? Do you know that nothing you do in this life will ever matter, unless it is about loving God and loving the people He has made?*

If the answer to those questions is yes, then let your bet match your talk. True faith means holding nothing back; it bets everything on the hope of eternity.

I know that this whole swimming-upstream, pursuing-Christ, taking-up-your-cross, counting-the-cost thing isn't easy. It's so hard, in

# when you're in love

*O God, I have tasted Thy goodness, and it has both satisfied
me and made me thirsty for more. I am painfully conscious
of my need for further grace. I am ashamed of my lack of
desire. O God, the Triune God, I want to want Thee; I long
to be filled with longing; I thirst to be made more thirsty still.
Show me Thy glory, I pray Thee, so that I may know Thee
indeed. Begin in mercy a new work of love within me. Say to
my soul, "Rise up my love, my fair one, and come away."
Then give me grace to rise and follow Thee up from this
misty lowland where I have wandered so long.[10]*

Have you ever met someone who was utterly and desperately in love with Jesus? I have. My wife's grandma Clara.

I spoke recently at Grandma Clara's funeral, and I could honestly tell the mourners gathered that I had never known anyone more excited to see Jesus. Every morning Clara would kneel by her bed and spend precious hours with her Savior and Lover; later in the day, just the sight of that corner of her bed would bring joy-filled tears and a deep anticipation of the next morning spent kneeling in His presence.

Grandma Clara acted toward God the way we act toward people we're madly in love with.

When you are truly in love, you go to great lengths to be with the one you love. You'll drive for hours to be together, even if it's only for a short while. You don't mind staying up late to talk. Walking in the rain is romantic, not annoying. You'll willingly spend a small fortune on the one you're crazy about. When you are apart from each other, it's painful, even miserable. He or she is all you think about; you jump at any chance to be together.

In his book *God Is the Gospel*, John Piper essentially asks whether we are in love with God:

> The critical question for our generation—and for every generation—is this: If you could have heaven, with no sickness, and with all the friends you ever had on earth, and all the food you ever liked, and all the leisure activities you ever enjoyed, and all the natural beauties you ever saw, all the physical pleasures you ever tasted, and no human conflict or

any natural disasters, could you be satisfied with heaven, if Christ was not there?[11]

How many of you will read those words and say, "You know, I just might be okay with that"? If you are as deeply in love with God as Grandma Clara was, you know you could never be satisfied in a heaven without Christ.

## Don't Try so Hard

My fear in writing the previous chapter is that it only evokes in you fear and guilt. Personal experience has taught me that actions driven by fear and guilt are not an antidote to lukewarm, selfish, comfortable living. I hope you realize instead that the answer is *love*.

Grandma Clara used to say, "I love love." Don't we all? Don't we crave it? And isn't that what God wants of us—to crave this relationship with Him as we crave all genuine love relationships? Isn't that what brings Him glory—when believers *desire* Him and are not merely slaves who serve Him out of obligation?

> You, my brothers, were *called to be free*. But do not use your freedom to indulge the sinful nature; rather, serve one another in love. The entire law is summed up in a single command: "Love your neighbor as yourself."
>
> —Galatians 5:13–14

Do you understand what this passage is saying? When we love, we're free! We don't have to worry about a burdensome load of commands, because when we are loving, we can't sin. Do you feel free in your Christian life?

In the same chapter, Paul writes, "The only thing that counts is faith expressing itself through love" (v. 6). Is loving God—and, by extension, loving people—what you are about? Is it what being a Christian means to you? Do you live as though faith, demonstrated through love, really is the only thing that counts?

For a long time, I sure didn't. And most of the people I knew were the same way.

There is so often a great disparity between how we feel about faith and how we are meant to feel. Why do so few people genuinely find joy and pleasure in their relationship with God? Why do most people feel they have to either pay God back for all He's done (buy His love) or somehow keep making up for all their inadequacies and failures (prove their love)? Why are the words of Psalm 63:1–5 not an honest reflection of our lives on most days?

O God, you are my God, earnestly I seek you; my soul thirsts for you, my body longs for you, in a dry and weary land where there is no water. I have seen you in the sanctuary and beheld your power and your glory. Because your love is better than life, my lips will glorify you. I will praise you as long as I live, and in your name I will lift up my hands. My soul will be satisfied as with the richest of foods; with singing lips my mouth will praise you.

Lukewarm living and claiming Christ's name simultaneously is utterly disgusting to God. And when we are honest, we have to admit that it isn't very fulfilling or joyful to us, either.

But the solution isn't to try harder, fail, and then make bigger promises, only to fail again. It does no good to muster up more love for God, to will yourself to love Him more. When loving Him becomes obligation, one of many things we have to do, we end up focusing even more on ourselves. No wonder so few people want to hear from us about what we ourselves feel is a boring, guilt-ridden chore!

As I wrote in the last chapter, we are called to surrender everything for Christ—a concept most churchgoers are not particularly thrilled by. So what is missing? What's wrong with this picture? Are we just fooling ourselves that we really can be in love with God and that it is more satisfying than anything else? I don't believe so.

## Help! I Don't Love You

God wants to change us; He died so that we could change.

The answer lies in *letting* Him change you. Remember His counsel to the lukewarm church in Laodicea? "Here I am! I stand at the door and knock. If anyone hears my voice and opens the door, I will come in and eat with him, and he with me" (Rev. 3:20). His counsel wasn't to "try harder," but rather to let Him in. As James wrote, "Come near to God and he will come near to you" (4:8).

Jesus Christ didn't die only to save us from hell; He also died to save us from our bondage to sin. In John 10:10, Jesus says, "I have come that they may have life, and have it to the full." He wasn't talking about the future. He meant now, in this lifetime.

The fact is, I need God to help me love God. And if I need His help to love Him, a perfect being, I definitely need His help to love other, fault-filled humans. Something mysterious, even supernatural must happen in order for genuine love for God to grow in our hearts. The Holy Spirit has to move in our lives.

It is a remarkable cycle: Our prayers for more love result in love, which naturally causes us to pray more, which results in more love …

Imagine going for a run while eating a box of Twinkies. Besides being self-defeating and sideache-inducing, it would also be near impossible—you would have to stop running in order to eat the Twinkies.

In the same way, you have to stop loving and pursuing Christ in order to sin. When you are pursuing love, running toward Christ, you do not have opportunity to wonder, *Am I doing this right?* or *Did I serve enough this week?* When you are running toward Christ, you are freed up to serve, love, and give thanks without guilt, worry, or fear. As long as you are running, you are safe.

But running is exhausting—if, that is, we are running from sin or guilt, out of fear. (Or if we haven't run in a while.) However, if we train ourselves to run toward our Refuge, toward Love, we are free—just as we are called to be.

As we begin to focus more on Christ, loving Him and others becomes more natural. As long as we are pursuing Him, we are satisfied in Him. It is when we stop actively loving Him that we find ourselves restless and gravitating toward other means of fulfillment.

When I read the psalms, I witness an extreme intimacy that at times seems unattainable. I have to remind myself constantly that the psalms were written by people just like me. They enjoyed closeness with God that you and I can experience. We should be communicating these words to Him:

> Like a weaned child with its mother, like a weaned child is my soul within me. (Ps. 131:2)

> You have filled my heart with greater joy than when their grain and new wine abound. I will lie down and sleep in peace, for you alone, O LORD, make me dwell in safety. (Ps. 4:7–8)

> You have made known to me the path of life; you will fill me with joy in your presence, with eternal pleasures at your right hand. (Ps. 16:11)

> The LORD is my strength and my shield; my heart trusts in him, and I am helped. My heart leaps for joy and I will give thanks to him in song. (Ps. 28:7)

> Satisfy us in the morning with your unfailing love, that we may sing for joy and be glad all our days. (Ps. 90:14)

Your statutes are my heritage forever; they are the joy of my heart. (Ps. 119:111)

I don't want to make it sound deceptively easy; the psalms are also filled with cries of pain:

Hear my prayer, O LORD, listen to my cry for help; be not deaf to my weeping. (Ps. 39:12)

Out of the depths I cry to you, O LORD; O Lord, hear my voice. Let your ears be attentive to my cry for mercy. (Ps. 130:1–2)

Jesus said, "In this world *you will have trouble*. But take heart! I have overcome the world" (John 16:33). Life isn't perfect when you follow Christ wholeheartedly; you will have trouble, Jesus says—it is pretty much guaranteed.

*But* He has overcome the world. So take heart, keep on, fight the good fight, pray continuously, and do not grow weary. There is nothing better than giving up everything and stepping into a passionate love relationship with God, the God of the universe who made galaxies, leaves, laughter, and me and you.

↓↑

*So what if I do believe that He has overcome the world? Until His kingdom comes, what about the sin I can't seem to escape? What about my messed-up family? What about my past? What about my grandma's cancer? What about the car accident that killed my friend? What about the divorce?*

We each have a list that goes on and on.

The promise that our troubles are "achieving for us an eternal glory" seems hard to believe in the midst of the mess. It sounds trite to say that our struggles on this earth are "light and momentary," as Paul wrote, doesn't it? Mine don't feel that way. At times they threaten to engulf the rest of my life.

Yet God tells us that we are getting the better end of the deal, that we really will be rewarded in a manner that far outweighs our current frustrations and hardships. And even that we are blessed "when men hate you, when they exclude you and insult you and reject your name as evil, because of the Son of Man. Rejoice in that day and leap for joy, because great is your reward in heaven" (Luke 6:22–23).

> They called the apostles in and had them flogged. Then they ordered them not to speak in the name of Jesus, and let them go. The apostles left the Sanhedrin, rejoicing because they had been counted worthy of suffering disgrace for the Name. Day after day, in the temple courts and from house to house,

they never stopped teaching and proclaiming the good news
that Jesus is the Christ.

—Acts 5:40–42

Wow. I hope that if I'm ever in a similar situation, I'll rejoice like
the apostles did. But I sometimes think I would more likely lament my
situation and get upset at God.

When I look at my relationship with God as a chore, a sacrifice, then
*I* am getting the glory—not God. I keep saying, "Look what I have sacrificed for God.…" or "Listen to what I do for God. It's hard, exhausting
really.…"

Instead, when we sacrifice, give, and even suffer, we can rejoice because
we know that God rewards us. We are always the recipients of His great
and manifold gifts. Not the givers. Never the givers. David Livingston, a
missionary to Africa during the 1800s, once said during a speech to students at Cambridge University, "People talk of the sacrifice I have made
in spending so much of my life in Africa.… I never made a sacrifice. We
ought not to talk of 'sacrifice' when we remember the great sacrifice which
He made who left His Father's throne on high to give Himself for us."[12]

The God who made the world and everything in it is the
Lord of heaven and earth and does not live in temples built
by hands. And he is not served by human hands, as if he
needed anything, because he himself gives all men life and
breath and everything else.

—Acts 17:24–25

The Bible says that when we obey God's commands, we benefit. I think we naturally assume that if we look out for our own interests and concerns, we will be happy. But people who sacrifice for others will tell you that seasons of giving are the most rewarding of their lives.

It turns out that the Bible is right—"It is better to give than to receive" (Acts 20:35). People generally do find greater joy in giving freely to others than they do in rampant self-indulgence. Regarding this, the playwright George Bernard Shaw writes, "This is true joy in life, the being used up for a purpose recognized by yourself as a mighty one; the being a force of nature instead of a feverish, selfish little clod of ailments and grievances complaining that the world will not devote itself to making you happy."

God is the only true Giver, and He needs nothing from us. But still He wants us. He gave us life so that we might seek and know Him.

## Jesus: Servant, Not Beggar

In Malachi 1:11 (NASB), God says, "From the rising of the sun even to its setting, My name will be great among the nations, and in every place incense is going to be offered to My name, and a grain offering that is pure; for My name will be great among the nations."

God tells the priests that if they don't want to give Him excellence, others will. God says His name will be great among the nations. Right now a hundred million angels are praising God's name; He certainly doesn't need to beg or plead with us. We should be the ones begging to worship in His presence.

Later in Malachi, we get an incredible promise from God: "'Bring the whole tithe into the storehouse, so that there may be food in My house, and test Me now in this,' says the LORD of hosts, 'if I will not open for you the windows of heaven and pour out for you a blessing until it overflows'" (Mal. 3:10 NASB).

This is the only place in the Bible where God invites His people to test Him, to try to out-give Him. He knows it is impossible, that no one can out-give the One from whom all things come. God knows people will realize that "we have given you only what comes from your hand" (1 Chron. 29:14). Nothing has strengthened my faith more than seeing God bless what I give back to Him, what I surrender at His feet.

If you really want to experience God's supernatural provision, then do as He says. Test Him. Give more than you can manage, and see how He responds.

When we are focused on loving Christ, it doesn't mean we do less. I used to do many of the same things I do now, but I was motivated by guilt or fear of consequences. When we work for Christ out of obligation, it *feels* like work. But when we truly love Christ, our work is a manifestation of that love, and it feels like love.

In reality, not one of us will ever be worthy. It *is* useless to attempt earning it; you will never feel ready. It is unknown and uncomfortable. But there really is a God who forgives everything and loves endlessly.

## SomeOne I Can Be Real With

If you merely pretend that you enjoy God or love Him, He knows. You can't fool Him; don't even try.

Instead, tell Him how you feel. Tell Him that He isn't the most important thing in this life to you, and that you're sorry for that. Tell Him that you've been lukewarm, that you've chosen _____ over Him time and again. Tell Him that you want Him to change you, that you long to genuinely enjoy Him. Tell Him how you want to experience true satisfaction and pleasure and joy in your relationship with Him. Tell Him you want to love Him more than anything on this earth. Tell Him you want to treasure the kingdom of heaven so much that you'd willingly sell everything in order to get it. Tell Him what you like about Him, what you appreciate, and what brings you joy.

*Jesus, I need to give myself up. I am not strong enough to love You and walk with You on my own. I can't do it, and I need You. I need You deeply and desperately. I believe You are worth it, that You are better than anything else I could have in this life or the next. I want You. And when I don't, I want to want You. Be all in me. Take all of me. Have Your way with me.*

# your best life... later

By now you've probably realized that you have a distinct choice to make: just let life happen, which is tantamount to serving God your leftovers, or actively run toward Christ.

Do you recognize the foolishness of seeking fulfillment outside of Him? Do you understand that it's impossible to please God in any way other than wholehearted surrender? Do you grasp the beauty and deep joy of walking in genuine intimacy with God, our holy Father and Friend? Do you want to see God more than you desire security?

Maybe you answered yes to these questions but still wonder what that equates to, what the alternatives are to floating downstream or riding down the escalator. What does running toward Christ and pursuing Love look like in daily life?

The best place I know to look is in Scripture; here we gather wisdom and study the examples of those who followed God wholeheartedly. The best passage is probably Hebrews 11, a chapter often called the "hall of faith." It is tempting to assume that the people listed there were superhuman, or supersaints, and that you and I could never do the kinds of things they did.

But did you know that Abraham was afraid for his safety, so he lied about his wife, Sarah, and said that she was his sister … twice? Consider Jacob, who stole his brother Esau's birthright, tricked his father into blessing him, and then fled in fear from Esau.

Or did you know that Moses was a murderer and so scared of speaking up that God had to send his brother, Aaron, to be Moses' mouthpiece? Also in Hebrews 11 we see Rahab, who was a Gentile and a woman (in that time, a serious disadvantage), not to mention a prostitute! Then there's Samson, who had so many issues I don't even know where to begin. And of course, David, a "man after God's own heart" who was an adulterer and a murderer, whose children were evil and out of control.

These people were far from perfect, yet they had faith in a God who was able to come through in seemingly dire situations. For example, Noah, who "by faith … when warned about things not yet seen, in holy fear built an ark to save his family. By his faith he condemned the world and became heir of the righteousness that comes by faith" (Heb. 11:7). Noah spent 120 years building an ark and warning others of the impending judgment. Suppose the flood had never come—Noah would have been the biggest laughingstock on earth. Having faith often means doing what others see as crazy. Something is wrong when our lives make sense to unbelievers.

And then there's Abraham. Hebrews 11:17–19 says,

> By faith Abraham, when God tested him, offered Isaac as a sacrifice. He who had received the promises was about to sacrifice his one and only son, even though God had said to him, "It is through Isaac that your offspring will be reckoned." Abraham reasoned that God could raise the dead, and figuratively speaking, he did receive Isaac back from death.

Abraham's hope lay in God's ability to raise the dead. What if God hadn't stopped Abraham? Imagine standing over your dead son after killing him. What would run through your mind as you buried your child? Could you go on living as everyone called you an insane murderer? These would have been the consequences of Abraham's actions if God did not come through. But He did.

Finally, think about the martyrs. Hebrews 11:35–38 says,

> [They] were tortured and refused to be released, so that they might gain a better resurrection. Some faced jeers and flogging, while still others were chained and put in prison. They were stoned; they were sawed in two; they were put to death by the sword. They went about in sheepskins and goatskins, destitute, persecuted and mistreated—the world was not

worthy of them. They wandered in deserts and mountains, and in caves and holes in the ground.

If eternity doesn't come and God does not exist, then, as Paul says, "If only for this life we have hope in Christ, we are to be pitied more than all men" (1 Cor. 15:19). If there is no God, then Paul and all the martyrs throughout history lived short lives full of needless suffering (2 Cor. 6:4–10).

But since God *is* real, Paul and the martyrs should be envied more than all people; their suffering was worth it. If we allow ourselves to live recklessly for Him, then we, too, will see His glory. We will see Him do the impossible.

Christians today like to play it safe. We want to put ourselves in situations where we are safe "even if there is no God." But if we truly desire to please God, we cannot live that way. We have to do things that cost us during our life on earth but will be more than worth it in eternity.

As chronicled in Hebrews 11, the God that the people of faith served is the very One we serve. As James 5:17 says, "Elijah was a man just like us." When you pray, your prayers are heard by the same God who answered Moses' prayer for water in the desert, the God who gave Abraham and his barren wife a son, and the God who made the slave Joseph second in power only to Pharaoh.

↓↑

The ultimate example of sacrifice and surrender is, of course, Jesus Christ. He had everything and still chose to surrender it out of love for His Father. Your attitude should be the same as His ...

> Who, being in very nature God, did not consider equality with God something to be grasped, but made himself nothing, taking the very nature of a servant, being made in human likeness. And being found in appearance as a man, he humbled himself and became obedient to death—even death on a cross! Therefore God exalted him to the highest place and gave him the name that is above every name, that at the name of Jesus every knee should bow, in heaven and on earth and under the earth, and every tongue confess that Jesus Christ is Lord, to the glory of God the Father.
>
> —Philippians 2:6–11

John clearly tells us that "whoever claims to live in him must walk as Jesus did" (1 John 2:6). Are you ready and willing to make yourself nothing? To take the very nature of a servant? To be obedient unto death? If your honest answer to those questions is yes, how are those intentions manifested in your life?

In Matthew 25 we get a frightening picture of the coming judgment. In this passage, Christ condemns people to eternal punishment because they did not care for Him during their lives on earth. "I was hungry and you gave me nothing to eat, I was thirsty and you gave me nothing to drink, I was a stranger and you did not invite me in, I needed clothes and you did not clothe me, I was sick and in prison and you did not look after me" (vv. 42–43).

The condemned protest, saying they never saw Christ in any of these positions of need, and Jesus responds, "I tell you the truth, whatever you did not do for one of the least of these, you did not do for me" (v. 45).

*Ouch.* To me that is like a stinging, unexpected slap in the face. Like many of you, I've heard that passage taught on numerous occasions. I've left convicted, but haven't taken it literally. We see it as a fresh perspective on poverty rather than a literal picture of impending judgment.

How would my life change if I actually thought of each person I came into contact with as Christ—the person driving painfully slow in front of me, the checker at the grocery store who seems more interested in chatting than ringing up my items, the member of my own family with whom I can't seem to have a conversation and not get annoyed?

If we believe that, as Jesus said, the two greatest commands are to "love the Lord your God with all your heart, soul, and mind" and to "love your neighbor as yourself," then this passage has a lot to teach us. Basically, Christ is connecting the command to "love God" with the command to "love your neighbor." By loving "the least of these," we are loving God Himself.

In this same chapter of Matthew, Jesus blesses some people for what they have done. Confused, they ask, "Lord, when did we see you hungry and feed you, or thirsty and give you something to drink? When did we see you a stranger and invite you in, or needing clothes and clothe you? When did we see you sick or in prison and go to visit you?" (vv. 37–39).

His answer is staggering: "The King will reply, 'I tell you the truth, whatever you did for one of the least of these brothers of mine, you did for me'" (v. 40). Jesus is saying that we show tangible love for God in how we care for the poor and those who are suffering. He expects us to treat the poor and the desperate as if they were Christ Himself.

Ask yourself this: If you actually saw Jesus starving, what would you do for Him?

> This is how we know what love is: Jesus Christ laid down his life for us. And we ought to lay down our lives for our brothers. If anyone has material possessions and sees his brother in need but has no pity on him, how can the love of God be in him? Dear children, let us not love with words or tongue but with actions and in truth. This then is how we know that we belong to the truth, and how we set our hearts at rest in his presence whenever our hearts condemn us.
>
> —1 John 3:16–20

In this passage, we see that John questions whether it is possible to truly have God's love in you if you have no compassion for the poor. He uses as his example Christ's love manifesting itself through the sacrifice of His very life.

God didn't just give a little for us; He gave His best. He gave Himself. John is saying that it is no different for us: True love requires sacrifice. And our love is shown by how we live our lives: "Let us not love with words or tongue but with actions and in truth."

One of the clearest ways we love "with actions and in truth" is through giving to others. By giving, I don't mean just money, although that is certainly an element of it.

Another important element of giving is with our time. Most of us are so busy that the thought of adding one more thing to our weekly schedule is stressful. Instead of adding in another thing to our lives, perhaps God wants us to give Him all of our time and let Him direct it as He sees fit. One of the most memorized verses in the whole Bible says, "For God so loved the world that he gave" (John 3:16). Right there we see the connection between loving and giving evidently established.

Giving that is not motivated by love is worth nothing. Paul says from this kind of giving we "gain nothing"; however, when we give out of love, we gain much. Giving results not only in heavenly compensation, but also gives us great joy in our lives here and now. As we love more genuinely and deeply, giving becomes the obvious and natural response. Taking and keeping for ourselves becomes unattractive and imprudent.

Remember the story where Jesus fed thousands of people with one boy's small lunch? In that story, according to Matthew, Jesus gave the loaves to His disciples and then the disciples passed them out to the crowd. Imagine if the disciples had simply held onto the food Jesus gave them, continually thanking Him for providing lunch for them. That would've been stupid when there was enough food to feed the thousands who were gathered and hungry.

But that is exactly what we do when we fail to give freely and joyfully. We are loaded down with too many good things, more than we could ever need, while others are desperate for a small loaf. The good things we cling to are more than money; we hoard our resources, our gifts, our time, our families, our friends. As we begin to practice regular giving, we see how ludicrous it is to hold on to the abundance God has given us and merely repeat the words *thank you.*

The apostle Paul addresses this issue of giving in light of the inequalities among the early believers:

> Our desire is not that others might be relieved while you are hard pressed, but that there might be equality. At the present time your plenty will supply what they need, so that in turn their plenty will supply what you need. Then there will be equality, as it is written: "He who gathered much did not have too much, and he who gathered little did not have too little."
>
> —2 Corinthians 8:13–15

Paul was asking the Corinthian believers to give to the impoverished saints in Jerusalem, the goal being that no one would have too much or too little. This idea is pretty far-fetched in modern-day culture, where we are taught to look out for ourselves and are thus rewarded.

The gap is so extreme in our world that we have to take lightly passages such as Luke 12:33: "Sell your possessions and give to the poor." How else can I walk out of a mud shack and back into my two-thousand-square-foot house without doing anything? The concept of downsizing so that others might upgrade is biblical, beautiful ... and nearly unheard of. We either close the gap or don't take the words of the Bible literally.

Dare to imagine what it would mean for you to take the words of Jesus seriously. Dare to think about your own children living in poverty, without enough to eat. Dare to believe that those really are your brothers and sisters in need.

Jesus said, "Whoever does the will of my Father in heaven is my brother and sister and mother" (Matt. 12:50). Do you believe that? Do you live like you believe it?

After hearing this truth preached, a guy at my church donated his house to the church and moved in with his parents. He told me that he will have a better house in heaven, and that it doesn't really matter where he lives during this lifetime. He is living like he believes.

Dream a little about what that might look like for you. Perhaps you start a movement called Aspiring to the Median, where people commit to living at or below the median U.S. income ($46,000 in 2006) and giving the rest away. Is it intimidating to think about giving radically and liberally?

I want to share a story with you. Anyone who has ever taken God at His word when He says, "Test me in this … and see if I will not … pour out so much blessing that you will not have room enough for it" (Mal. 3:10) probably has a similar tale.

A friend was faithfully giving 20 percent of his income to God, and suddenly his income dropped drastically. He knew he had to decide whether he should continue to give in a way that proved he trusted God. It wouldn't have been wrong to lower his giving to 10 percent. But my friend chose *instead* to increase his giving to 30 percent, despite the income reduction.

You can probably guess how the story ends. God blessed his faith and gave him more than enough, more than he needed. My friend got to experience God's provision firsthand.

When it's hard and you are doubtful, give more. Or, as Deuteronomy says, "Give liberally and be ungrudging when you do so, for on this account the LORD your God will bless you in all your work and in all that you undertake" (15:10 NRSV).

Maybe you have already made sacrifices. If so, you have seen that in some ways it gets easier, doesn't it? You have witnessed the benefits of giving and are blessed because of it. But it gets harder, too. The temptation to level off increases with each passing year. Pride tells you that you've sacrificed more than others. Fear tells you it's time to worry about the future. Friends say you've given enough, that it's someone else's turn now.

But Jesus says to keep on and you will see more of God. Do we really believe that "it ought to be the business of every day to prepare for our final day"?[13]

When Jesus sent out His twelve disciples (Luke 9:3), He told them to "take nothing for the journey—no staff, no bag, no bread, no money, no extra tunic." Why do you suppose He said this? Why not let them run home and grab a few supplies? Why not allow them to bring some money along just in case?

Jesus was forcing His disciples to trust Him. God would have to come through for them because they had nothing else to fall back on.

This place of trust isn't a comfortable place to be; in fact, it flies in the face of everything we've been taught about proper planning. We like finding refuge in what we already have rather than in what we hope God will provide. But when Christ says to count the cost of following Him, it means we must surrender everything. It means being willing to go without an extra tunic or a place to sleep at night, and sometimes without knowing where we are going.

God wants us to trust Him with abandon. He wants to show us how He works and cares for us. He wants to be our refuge.

↓↑

Walking in genuine intimacy and full surrender to God requires great faith. Hebrews 11:6 says, "Without faith it is impossible to please God, because anyone who comes to him must believe that he exists and that he rewards those who earnestly seek him."

Back when I was in Bible college, a professor asked our class, "What are you doing right now that requires faith?" That question affected me deeply because at the time I could think of nothing in my life that required faith. I probably wouldn't be living very differently if I didn't believe in God; my life was neither ordered nor affected by my faith like I had assumed it was. Furthermore, when I looked around, I realized I was surrounded by people who lived the same way I did.

Life is comfortable when you separate yourself from people who are different from you. That epitomizes what my life was like: characterized by comfort.

But God doesn't call us to be comfortable. He calls us to trust Him so completely that we are unafraid to put ourselves in situations where we will be in trouble if He doesn't come through.

Even though chapter 58 of Isaiah was written thousands of years ago, it speaks powerfully to the present day. I know it's long, but it is well worth the read, I promise.

"For day after day they seek me out; they seem eager to know my ways, as if they were a nation that does what is right and has not forsaken the commands of its God. They ask me for just decisions and seem eager for God to come near them. 'Why have we fasted,' they say, 'and you have not seen it? Why have we humbled ourselves, and you have not noticed?'

"Yet on the day of your fasting, you do as you please and exploit all your workers. Your fasting ends in quarreling and strife, and in striking each other with wicked fists. You cannot fast as you do today and expect your voice to be heard on high. Is this the kind of fast I have chosen, only a day for a man to humble himself? Is it only for bowing one's head like a reed and for lying on sackcloth and ashes? Is that what you call a fast, a day acceptable to the LORD?

"Is not this the kind of fasting I have chosen: to loose the chains of injustice and untie the cords of the yoke, to set the oppressed free and break every yoke? Is it not to share your food with the hungry and to provide the poor wanderer with shelter—when you see the naked, to clothe him, and not to turn away from your own flesh and blood? Then your light will break forth like the dawn, and your healing will quickly appear; then your righteousness will go before you, and the glory of the LORD will be your rear guard. Then you will call, and the LORD will answer; you will cry for help, and he will say: Here am I.

"If you do away with the yoke of oppression, with the pointing finger and malicious talk, and if you spend yourselves in behalf of the hungry and satisfy the needs of the oppressed, then your light will rise in the darkness, and your night will become like the noonday. The LORD will guide you always; he will satisfy your needs in a sun-scorched land and will strengthen your frame. You will be like a well-watered garden, like a spring whose waters never fail. Your people will rebuild the ancient ruins and will raise up the age-old foundations; you will be called Repairer of Broken Walls, Restorer of Streets with Dwellings.

"If you keep your feet from breaking the Sabbath and from doing as you please on my holy day, if you call the Sabbath a delight and the LORD's holy day honorable, and if you honor it by not going your own way and not doing as you please or speaking idle words, then you will find your joy in the LORD, and I will cause you to ride on the heights of the

land and to feast on the inheritance of your father Jacob."
The mouth of the LORD has spoken.

—Isaiah 58:2–14

In verse 10, the phrase "if you spend yourselves" stands out to me even more than the amazing promises that follow. It reminds me of the parable of the talents in Matthew 25, wherein the servants are rewarded according to what they did with what they were given. It didn't seem to matter that one was given five talents and the other two. Both servants were faithful with what their master entrusted to them, and as a result both were rewarded liberally.

Similarly, we are each given different gifts and talents by our Master. The thing that matters most is how we use what we have been given, not how much we make or do compared to someone else. What matters is that we spend ourselves.

And now, little children, abide in him, so that when he appears we may have confidence and not shrink from him in shame at his coming.

—1 John 2:28 RSV

# profile of the obsessed

**Obsessed:** *To have the mind excessively preoccupied with a single emotion or topic.*[14]

The idea of holding back certainly didn't come from Scripture. The Bible teaches us to be consumed with Christ and to faithfully live out His words. The Holy Spirit stirs in us a joy and peace when we are fixated on Jesus, living by faith, and focused on the life to come.

## Lovers

I think sometimes we assume that if we are nice, people will know that we are Christians and want to know more about Jesus. But it really doesn't work that way. I know a lot of people who don't know Christ and are really nice people—nicer and more fun to be with, in fact, than a lot of Christians I know.

There has to be more to our faith than friendliness, politeness, and even kindness. Jesus teaches in Luke's gospel:

> If you love those who love you, what credit is that to you? Even "sinners" love those who love them. And if you do good to those who are good to you, what credit is that to you? Even "sinners" do that. And if you lend to those from whom you expect repayment, what credit is that to you? Even "sinners" lend to "sinners," expecting to be repaid in full. But love your enemies, do good to them, and lend to them without expecting to get anything back. Then your reward will be great, and you will be sons of the Most High, because he is kind to the ungrateful and wicked. Be merciful, just as your Father is merciful.
>
> —Luke 6:32–36

True faith is loving a person after he has hurt you. True love makes you stand out.

In October 2006, near Lancaster, Pennsylvania, a man stormed an Amish school and killed several girls. The day after the shootings, many

Amish people visited the shooter's family to say they had forgiven him. That sort of forgiveness is incomprehensible to the world; because of it, people have even accused the families of being bad parents, of not dealing properly with their anger, of living in denial.

It is just this sort of love that is crazy to the world: true love, a kind found nowhere but through Christ.

We are commanded to love our enemies and do good to them. Who are your enemies? Or, in terms we connect with better, who are the people you avoid or who avoid you? Who are the people who have hurt you or hurt your friends or hurt your kids? Are you willing to do good to those people? To reach out to them?

Oftentimes, my first response when someone does something to me—or worse, to my wife or to one of my kids—is retaliation. I don't *want* to bless those who hurt me or people I love dearly. I wouldn't *want* to forgive someone who walked into my daughter's school and shot her and her friends.

But that is exactly what Christ asks us to do. He commands that we give without expecting anything in return.

Later in Luke, Jesus says,

> When you give a luncheon or dinner, do not invite your friends, your brothers or relatives, or your rich neighbors; if you do, they may invite you back and so you will be repaid. But when you give a banquet, invite the poor, the crippled, the lame, the blind, and you will be blessed. Although they cannot repay you, you will be repaid at the resurrection of the righteous.
>
> —Luke 14:12–14

Have you ever actually done anything like that? Do you give to those who cannot repay you? To those who would do you harm, if they could? To those who have already done you harm? This is Christ's love. He gave us something for which we can *never* repay Him, and then He asks us to keep giving like He gives.

Frederick Buechner writes in *The Magnificent Defeat*,

The love for equals is a human thing—of friend for friend, brother for brother. It is to love what is loving and lovely. The world smiles. The love for the less fortunate is a beautiful thing—the love for those who suffer, for those who are poor, the sick, the failures, the unlovely. This is compassion, and it touches the heart of the world. The love for the more fortunate is a rare thing—to love those who succeed where we fail, to rejoice without envy with those who rejoice, the love of the poor for the rich, of the black man for the white man. The world is always bewildered by its saints. And then there is the love for the enemy—love for the one who does not love you but mocks, threatens, and inflicts pain. The tortured's love for the torturer. This is God's love. It conquers the world.

People who are **obsessed** with Jesus give freely and openly, without censure. Obsessed people love those who hate them and who can never love them back.

## Risk Takers

Haven't we all prayed the following prayer? *Lord, we pray for safety as we travel. We ask that no one gets hurt on this trip. Please keep everyone safe until we return, and bring us back safely. In Jesus' name we pray, amen.* The exact wording may vary a bit, but that is the standard prayer we recite before leaving on mission trips, retreats, vacations, and business trips.

We are consumed by safety. Obsessed with it, actually. Now, I'm not saying it is wrong to pray for God's protection, but I am questioning how we've made safety our highest priority. We've elevated safety to the neglect of whatever God's best is, whatever would bring God the most glory, or whatever would accomplish His purposes in our lives and in the world.

Would you be willing to pray this prayer? *God, bring me closer to You during this trip, whatever it takes....*

People who are **obsessed** with Jesus aren't consumed with their personal safety and comfort above all else. Obsessed people care more about God's kingdom coming to this earth than their own lives being shielded from pain or distress.

## Friends of All

Awhile back I had a free evening, so I decided to go to the store and buy some items to give away to those who needed them more than I do. It was a good idea, something I want my life to be characterized by more and more.

But it was embarrassing.

I realized that everyone I knew had enough, that I didn't know many people who were truly in need, and that I needed to change that. I needed to go and intentionally meet people who don't live like I do or think like I do, people who could never repay me. For their sake, but for my own as well.

First Timothy reaffirms that we are not to be controlled by money or to pursue it:

> Godliness with contentment is great gain. For we brought nothing into the world, and we can take nothing out of it. But if we have food and clothing, we will be content with that. People who want to get rich fall into temptation and a trap and into many foolish and harmful desires that plunge men into ruin and destruction. For the love of money is a root of all kinds of evil. Some people, eager for money, have wandered from the faith and pierced themselves with many griefs. But you, man of God, flee from all this, and pursue righteousness, godliness, faith, love, endurance and gentleness. Fight the good fight of the faith. Take hold of the eternal life to which you were called when

you made your good confession in the presence of many witnesses.

—1 Timothy 6:6–13

People who are **obsessed** with Jesus live lives that connect them with the poor in some way or another. Obsessed people believe that Jesus talked about money and the poor so often because it was really important to Him (1 John 2:4–6; Matt. 16:24–26).

## Crazy Ones

Sometimes I feel like when I make decisions that are remotely biblical, people who call themselves Christians are the first to criticize and say I'm crazy, that I'm taking the Bible too literally, or that I'm not thinking about my family's well-being.

For example, when I returned from my first trip to Africa, I felt very strongly that we were to sell our house and move into something smaller, in order to give more away. The feedback I got was along the lines of "It's not fair to your kids," "It's not a prudent financial choice," and "You are doing it just for show." I do not remember a single person who encouraged me to explore it or supported the decision at the time.

We ended up moving into a house half the size of our previous home, and we haven't regretted it. My response to the cynics, in the context of eternity, was, am I the crazy one for selling my house? Or are *you* for not giving more, serving more, being with your Creator more?

If one person "wastes" away his day by spending hours connecting with God, and the other person believes he is too busy or has better things to do than worship the Creator and Sustainer, who is the crazy one? If one person invests her or his resources in the poor—which, according to Matthew 25, is giving to Jesus Himself—and the other extravagantly remodels a temporary dwelling that will not last beyond his few years left on this earth, who is the crazy one?

When people gladly sacrifice their time or comfort or home, it is obvious that they trust in the promises of God. Why is it that the story of someone who has actually done what Jesus commands resonates deeply with us, but we then assume we could never do anything so radical or intense? Or why do we call it radical when, to Jesus, it is simply the way it is? The way it should be?

**Obsessed** people are more concerned with obeying God than doing what is expected or fulfilling the status quo. A person who is obsessed with Jesus will do things that don't always make sense in terms of success or wealth on this earth. As Martin Luther put it, "There are two days on my calendar: this day and that day" (Luke 14:25–35; Matt. 7:13–23; 8:18–22; Rev. 3:1–6).

## The Humble

The church in America loves to turn saints into celebrities, to make known the stories of humble people who have faithfully served Christ in some way. And there is much good that comes of that. In fact, in the next chapter we'll look closely at some examples.

But there can be a tragic consequence to it: Too many of these people fall for the praise and start to believe that they really are something special.

I spoke at a summer camp several years ago. Afterward, a number of students told me I was their "favorite speaker." It felt good to hear them talk about how funny and convicting my messages were. I loved it. I got back to my room and thanked God for helping me speak so well.

About three minutes into my prayer, I stopped. It hit me that the students were talking about *me*, not God. I was standing before a holy God and robbing Him of the glory that was rightfully His.

That's a terrifying position to find yourself in. God says, "I am the LORD; that is my name! I will not give my glory to another or my praise to idols" (Isa. 42:8). I realized immediately that any attention I received belonged to God.

It's pride, plain and simple, that keeps me from giving God all the glory and keeping some of it for myself. It is a battle we all fight, in some form or another, some of us daily or even hourly.

One of the ways I know to fight against pride is through focused prayer. What I mean is that before you say one word to God, take a minute and imagine what it would be like to stand before His throne as you pray. Remember the visions of John, in Revelation, and Isaiah; remember the many accounts of people coming into God's presence and how it always caused the people to fall on their faces in terror. And then start to pray.

A person who is **obsessed** with Jesus knows that the sin of pride is always a battle. Obsessed people know that you can never be "humble enough," and so they seek to make themselves less known and Christ more known (Matt. 5:16).

## Servers

As I shared in previous chapters, I used to be driven by my fear of God. I also used to work hard to prove that I was committed to God. Now I have tremendous fear and awe of God, but that doesn't motivate me. Now I work hard to serve God, but it isn't to prove my devotion.

Now I think I'm actually in love. Maybe that sounds corny to you, but I can't think of a more appropriate way to say it.

If a guy were dating my daughter but didn't want to spend the gas money to come pick her up or refused to buy her dinner because it cost too much, I would question whether he were really in love with her. In the same way, I question whether many American churchgoers are really in love with God because they are so hesitant to do anything for Him.

People who are **obsessed** with Jesus do not consider service a burden. Obsessed people take joy in loving God by loving His people (Matt. 13:44; John 15:8).

## Givers

Tears come to my eyes when I think about some of God's people I have had the privilege to meet in the past few years. These are people with families, with dreams, people who are made in God's image as much as you and I are. And these people are suffering.

Many of them are sick, some even dying, as they live out their lives in dwellings that we would not consider good enough for our household pets. I am not exaggerating. Much of their daily hardship and suffering could be relieved with access to food, clean water, clothing, adequate shelter, or basic medical attention.

I believe that God wants His people, His church, to meet these needs. The Scriptures are filled with commands and references about caring for the poor and for those who cannot help themselves. The crazy part about God's heart is that He doesn't *just* ask us to give; He desires that we love those in need *as much as we love ourselves.* That is the core of the second greatest command, to "love your neighbor as yourself" (Matt. 22:39).

He is asking you to love as you would want to be loved if it were your child who was blind from drinking contaminated water; to love the way you would want to be loved if you were the homeless woman sitting outside the café; to love as though it were your family living in the shack slapped together from cardboard and scrap metal.

Non-churchgoers tend to see Christians as takers rather than givers. When Christians sacrifice and give wildly to the poor, that is truly a light that glimmers. The Bible teaches that the church is to be that light, that sign of hope, in an increasingly dark and hopeless world. Matthew 5:16 says, "Let your light shine before men, that they may see your good deeds and praise your Father in heaven."

> People who are **obsessed** with God
> are known as givers, not takers.

> Obsessed people genuinely think that others matter as much as they do, and they are particularly aware of those who are poor around the world (James 2:14–26).

## Sojourners

Most Americans, and even more so those of us in Southern California, think about life on earth way too much. Much of our time, energy, and money are channeled toward that which is temporary. Paul writes,

> For, as I have often told you before and now say again even with tears, many live as enemies of the cross of Christ. Their destiny is destruction, their god is their stomach, and their glory is in their shame. Their mind is on earthly things. But our citizenship is in heaven. And we eagerly await a Savior from there, the Lord Jesus Christ, who, by the power that enables him to bring everything under his control, will transform our lowly bodies so that they will be like his glorious body.
>
> —Philippians 3:18–21

As I said before, my wife's grandma Clara offered a real-life example of a person consumed with Jesus. I once attended a play with my wife and some of her relatives, including Grandma Clara. During intermission, I leaned over and asked what she thought of the play. She said, "Oh honey, I really don't want to be here right now." When I asked why, she replied, "I just don't know if this is where I want to be when Christ returns. I'd rather be helping someone or on my knees praying. I don't want Him to return and find me sitting in a theater."

I was shocked by her answer. Yes, we are called to "keep watch" (Matt. 24:42), but it's strange to see someone who takes that command, and so many others, seriously. In fact, it's more than strange—it's convicting.

A person who is **obsessed** thinks about heaven frequently. Obsessed people orient their lives around eternity; they are not fixed only on what is here in front of them.

## The Engrossed

Jesus didn't just pull the greatest command out of nowhere. He hearkened all the way back to the days of Moses, when God says to His people,

Hear, O Israel: The LORD our God, the LORD is one. Love the LORD your God with all your heart and with all your soul and with all your strength. These commandments that I give you today are to be upon your hearts. Impress them on your children. Talk about them when you sit at home and when you walk along the road, when you lie down and when you get up. Tie them as symbols on your hands and bind them on your foreheads. Write them on the doorframes of your houses and on your gates.

—Deuteronomy 6:4–9

In Moses' time, the heart was understood to be the seat of a person's emotions, the very center of his being, the place where decisions are made. The soul was considered the basis for a person's traits and qualities, or his personality. Strength refers to physical, mental, *and* spiritual strength.

So within this command to love God with "all your heart and with all your soul and with all your strength," every fiber of humanity is addressed. Our goal as people who follow Christ should be no less than becoming people who are madly in love with God.

A person who is **obsessed** is characterized by committed, settled, passionate love for God, above and before every other thing and every other being.

## Unguarded Ones

Before my wife and I got married I knew that I had to tell her everything about me, all the ways I'd messed up, all the things I'd done. She had to know what she was getting before she agreed to marry me. That conversation was not easy, but at the end of it, we still chose to be with each other, to commit our lives to one another.

I find myself acting differently with God. Often, when I pray, I will phrase my sentences in a way that makes me sound better. I will try to soften my sins, or touch up my true feelings before laying them before God. How foolish it is for me to be completely honest with my wife about my shortcomings, but try to fool God!

God wants us to be open with Him. He definitely doesn't want us to "season our wretchedness" as we would raw meat. He knows what we are, that we are disgusting, that all we are doing is trying to make ourselves feel better.

God desires true intimacy with each of us, and that comes only when we trust Him enough to be fully transparent and vulnerable.

People who are **obsessed** are raw with God; they do not attempt to mask the ugliness of their sins or their failures. Obsessed people don't put it on for God; He is their safe place, where they can be at peace.

## The Rooted

The average Christian in the United States spends ten minutes per day with God; meanwhile, the average American spends over four hours a day watching television.[15]

Perhaps TV is not your thing—maybe you don't even own one. But how about your time and your resources? How much of your money is spent on yourself, and how much is directed toward God's kingdom? How much of your time is dedicated to pursuing your life and your goals, and how much is focused on God's work and purposes?

God doesn't want religious duty. He doesn't want a distracted, half-hearted "Fine, I'll read a chapter … now are You happy?" attitude. God wants His Word to be a delight to us, so much so that we meditate on it day and night.

In Psalm 1, He promises that those who do so are "like a tree planted by streams of water, which yields its fruit in season and whose leaf does not wither. Whatever he does prospers" (v. 3).

People who are **obsessed** with God have an intimate relationship with Him. They are nourished by God's Word throughout the day because they know that forty minutes on Sunday is not enough to sustain them for a whole week, especially when they will encounter so many distractions and alternative messages.

## The Dedicated

Have you been in really good physical shape at some point in your life? If you aren't at that same level of fitness today, you probably know that it didn't "just happen"; you didn't lose your six-pack or your ability to run eight miles overnight. You stopped running regularly, or you quit lifting weights three times a week, or you started adding a couple of extra scoops of ice cream to your bowl. There are reasons that we are where we are and who we are, and they aren't random.

It is the same way with joy in our lives. We tend to think of joy as something that ebbs and flows depending on life's circumstances. But we don't just lose joy, as though one day we have it and the next it's gone, oh darn. Joy is something that we have to choose and then work for. Like the ability to run for an hour, it doesn't come automatically. It needs cultivation.

When life gets painful or doesn't go as we hoped, it's okay if a little of our joy seeps away. The Bible teaches that true joy is formed in the midst of the difficult seasons of life.

A person who is **obsessed** with Jesus is more concerned with his or her character than comfort. Obsessed people know that true joy doesn't depend on circumstances or environment; it is a gift that must be chosen and cultivated, a gift that ultimately comes from God (James 1:2–4).

## Sacrificers

We cannot start believing that we are indispensable to God. According to the psalmist,

> I have no need of a bull from your stall or of goats from your pens, for every animal of the forest is mine, and the cattle on a thousand hills. I know every bird in the mountains, and the creatures of the field are mine. If I were hungry I would not tell you, for the world is mine, and all that is in it.... Sacrifice thank offerings to God, fulfill your vows to the Most High.
>
> —Psalm 50:9–12, 14

There is no way we can contribute or add to God. He has everything and is complete. When we are in God's presence, all we can do is praise Him. Romans 11:35–36 says, "'Who has ever given to God, that God should repay him?' For from him and through him and to him are all things. To him be the glory forever! Amen.'"

A person who is **obsessed** with Jesus knows that the best thing he can do is be faithful to his Savior in every aspect of his life, continually saying "Thank You!" to God. An obsessed person knows

there can never be intimacy if he
is always trying to pay God back
or work hard enough to be worthy.
He revels in his role as child and
friend of God.

While these descriptions combined don't necessarily answer the question of what it looks like to be wholly surrendered to God, they represent important pieces of the puzzle. Hopefully you are beginning to imagine and pray about what this looks like in your own life.

# who really lives that way?

*Follow my example, as I follow the example of Christ.*
—1 Corinthians 11:1

The stories that follow are true. They tell of people who sought to live their lives fully surrendered to God. Some are still alive; others have finished their race. Their examples differ vastly from one another, but each bears the mark of a person distinctly transformed by the beauty and reality of God's love and the guidance of the Holy Spirit.

In His letter to the church in Sardis, Jesus said, "You have a reputation of being alive, but you are dead. Wake up! Strengthen what remains and is about to die…. Yet you have a few people in Sardis who have not soiled their clothes. They will walk with me, dressed in white, for they are worthy" (Rev. 3:1–2, 4–5).

Jesus commended the few who were faithful. Likewise, there are a few in every generation who offer examples worth following.

Will your name be among the few that follow?

## Nathan Barlow

A medical doctor who chose to utilize his skills in Ethiopia for more than sixty years, Nathan dedicated his life to helping people with mossy foot. Mossy foot is a debilitating condition primarily found in rural districts, on people who work in soil of volcanic origin. It causes swelling and ulcers in the feet and lower legs. The subsequent deformity, swelling, repeated ulcerations, and secondary infections make people with mossy foot social outcasts equivalent to lepers.[16]

I met Nathan shortly before he died. His daughter, Sharon Daly, attends my church and brought him to her home from Ethiopia when his health started to fail. After only a few weeks, he couldn't handle being in the States. The people he loved were still in Ethiopia, so his daughter flew him back home so he could spend his last days there.

Once, Nathan got a toothache, the pain of which was so intense that he had to fly away from the mission field to get medical attention. Nathan told the dentist that he didn't ever want to leave the mission field for the sake of his teeth again, so he had the dentist pull out *all* of his teeth and give him false ones so he wouldn't slow God's work in Ethiopia.

This amazing man was the first to help these outcasts, and he spent his life doing it. Yet he died quietly, without a lot of attention; no one really knew about him.

It surprised me that such a man of God would faithfully serve for so many years, despite minimal recognition. It is a beautiful thing to witness. The work Nathan started continues through his Web site, www.mossyfoot.com.

## Simpson Rebbavarapu

Simpson was given his English name when he arrived at a missionary-run orphanage around the age of four. His parents had not yet named him, which happens often among the younger children of poverty-stricken, lower-caste families in India.

Simpson's mother was married as a child bride around the age of thirteen, a practice still common in Indian villages. Simpson was her sixth child, and the women in the village gave her herbs to end her pregnancy so that she wouldn't have to stop working *and* have another mouth to feed. But the herbs didn't work.

Other villagers suggested that she try the "English medicine." But when she went to the doctor to have him abort her baby, he did not come to work that day. So Simpson was born, and eventually his parents took him to the orphanage because they knew he would have a better life there, including an opportunity to be educated.

Simpson believes that God has always had His hand on his life, because if it had been up to his mother, he would never have been born. Currently, Simpson splits his time between an orphanage that he started and an evangelism ministry that brings God's Word to illiterate villagers through audio Bibles.

When asked how he lives and where he gets a salary, he answered in the most simple and humble manner, "I live by faith.... I don't have a family or a wife, so what do I need a salary for?" He would rather have that money go to supporting another program to help people or to expose more people to the Word of God.

Simpson says that by living this way, he has to trust that God has His hand on his life and will keep taking care of him. He also says his dependence keeps him in prayer and close to God. To learn more about what Simpson does, check out www.beumin.org.

## Jamie Lang

When Jamie was twenty-three years old, she flew from the United States to Tanzania with $2,000 from her savings account. She planned to stay until she ran out of money, at which point she would come home.

Jamie was overwhelmed by all of the need that she encountered, so she started praying that God would allow her to make a radical difference in one person's life. After about six months, she met an eight-year-old girl at church who was carrying a baby on her back. Jamie learned that the baby's mother was dying from AIDS and that she was too weak to care for him. Jamie began to buy formula for the little boy, Junio, to provide him with the nutrition he desperately needed. At the time, he was half the size of a healthy baby.

Jamie fell in love with baby Junio. She wondered if she was being foolish—a barely twenty-four-year-old, single, white American entertaining thoughts of adopting a baby. Besides, she didn't even know if Tanzania allowed international adoptions. Eventually, she discovered that the country *didn't* allow international adoptions; however, because she had lived there for over six months, she could establish residency.

Before Junio's mom died from AIDS, she came to Jamie and said, "I have heard how you are taking care of my son, and I have never known such a love. I want to be saved." Just before she died, she said, "I know that my son is taken care of, and I will see him in heaven someday."

Jamie spent six months going through the adoption process and then five more months working with the American embassy to get Junio a visa. When she finally came home, she had been gone for a year and a half.

Junio is now five years old, totally healthy, and HIV negative. When Junio's mom was pregnant with him, she took a "morning-after pill" late in her pregnancy in order to abort him. But instead it induced premature labor, and because Junio was so small, no bleeding occurred during his birth. Thus, he did not contract HIV from his mother. What was intended to end his life, God used to save it.

Since adopting Junio, Jamie has gotten married, had a little girl, and is moving back to Tanzania with her family to work with Wycliffe to translate the Bible for a group that has never heard it before.

## Marva J. Dawn

Marva was born in Ohio in 1948. She is a lifelong scholar, having earned four masters degrees and a PhD. She is also a teaching fellow at Regent College in Vancouver, British Columbia, and is involved with the organization Christians Equipped for Ministry. Marva has written many books, is a gifted musician, and speaks to clergy and at conferences all over the world.

One of her books, *Unfettered Hope: A Call to Faithful Living in an Affluent Society*, specifically addresses what a faithful response looks like in our culture. Her life is a reflection of her belief that seemingly small acts of faithfulness can have a profound and significant impact on the world. All of the profits of her books go to support charities like Stand With Africa: A Campaign of Hope, which "supports African churches and communities as they withstand AIDS, banish hunger, and build peace."[17]

Marva and her husband live off his teacher's salary, which is not much. Despite Marva's many medical problems, she still refuses to take more money for herself. She cannot imagine spending to make her life more comfortable when so many people are desperate and dying throughout our world. She says that her 1980 Volkswagen Bug with its broken heater helps her focus more on prayer and to better identify with those in need.

## Rich Mullins

Rich was born in 1955 in Richmond, Indiana, the third of six children. He began to study music at a young age and wrote his first song on the piano when he was just four years old.

Rich attended a Quaker church growing up, which later influenced his songwriting. He got his start writing songs for big-name recording artists, but in 1985 he recorded his debut album. For the next twelve years he made music, toured, and ministered to thousands of people through his simple yet weighty lyrics. His two most well-known songs are "Awesome God" and "Step by Step." His songs have been covered by artists and bands like John Tesh, Rebecca St. James, Michael W. Smith, Amy Grant, Third Day, Caedmon's Call, and Jars of Clay.

Despite his success in the music industry, Rich often ruffled the feathers of Christian music culture. He didn't consider music to be his primary purpose in life; to him, it simply enabled him to pursue the higher calling of loving people: children, his neighbors, enemies, and non-Christians. Sometimes he showed up to his concerts unshaven and barefoot. To keep others from putting him on a pedestal, he often confessed his sins and failures in public.

In 1995, Rich moved to a Navajo reservation in Arizona to teach music to the children who lived there. Rich never knew how successfully his albums sold because the profits from his concerts and albums went directly to his church. They paid him a small salary and gave the rest of the money away.

In September of 1997, Rich and a friend were driving to a benefit concert in Wichita, Kansas, when their Jeep flipped. Both men were thrown from the car; Rich was killed when a passing semi swerved to miss the Jeep and accidentally hit him. He was forty-one years old.

## Rings

I don't know how old exactly Rings is, but he's definitely what you would call an old man. I also don't know where he was born or what his real name is; he simply goes by Rings. His home is the cab of his pickup, which he parks near downtown Ocean Beach, California. He is a chain smoker, an ex-convict, ex-addict, and ex-alcoholic.

Rings likes to say that if Jesus saved him, then Jesus is able to save anyone and everyone. So instead of using his monthly check to buy alcohol or a hotel room for himself, he spends all of it on food at the local supermarket. He transfers the food he buys to coolers in the back of his truck, then he drives to the beach and makes meals for his fellow homeless.

While preparing the food, Rings tells the gathering crowd about the freedom that Jesus brought into his life. He tells them that God is the One who told him to feed others with his money, and that it's because God loves each of them. This man gives everything he has to others—literally everything—because he knows he has nothing that wasn't given to him by God.

## Rachel Saint

Rachel was born in 1914 in Pennsylvania, the only daughter among eight children. Her father was a stained-glass artist and their family often had very little food growing up.

When Rachel was eighteen, a kind, wealthy, elderly woman took Rachel on a trip to Europe and offered to make Rachel her heiress if she would be her companion for the rest of her life. While Rachel contemplated it, she knew she couldn't accept the offer of a comfortable life spent sipping tea and conversing.

After twelve years working at a halfway house for alcoholics, Rachel enrolled in linguistics school and became a missionary with Wycliffe

Bible Translators in South America. She spent several years working with the Shapra Indians of Peru, but ultimately knew she was called to work with the Waorani Indians of Ecuador, who were notorious for spearing to death any outsiders immediately upon contact.

Eventually, Rachel was introduced to a Waorani woman, Dayuma, who agreed to teach Rachel the language of her people. For years Rachel studied the language and witnessed to Dayuma about Jesus Christ as she waited patiently for an opportunity to go to the Waorani without being killed. Rachel's own brother, Nate, a pilot for Mission Aviation Fellowship, had been killed by the Waorani people when they attacked him and four other missionaries. This only sharpened Rachel's desire to tell these people about the love of Christ.

After many years, Rachel finally went to meet and live with the Waorani people. She lived with them for twenty years. Over time, their culture of revenge and murder was transformed by hearing what they called "God's carvings" (the words of the Bible). The Waorani people became her family. They gave Rachel the Waorani name Nimu, which means "star."

Rachel eventually translated the New Testament into their language, and today she is buried with her people in Ecuador. At her funeral, a Waorani friend said, "She called us her brothers. She told us how to believe. Now she is in heaven.... God is building a house for all of us, and that's where we'll see Nimu again."

## George Mueller

George was born in Prussia in 1805 and was attending the University of Halle when he became a Christian. Up until then he had been infamous for his gambling debts, drunken stories, and escapades. But his life was transformed when he came to know Christ.

He finished school and left for England to be a preacher. He and his British wife eventually settled in Bristol, England, where they saw many orphans roaming the streets—uncared for, unfed, often sick, and virtually guaranteed death at a young age. At this time, writers like Charles Dickens and William Blake had not yet brought attention to the plight of these children, and nothing was being done to help them.

George and his wife decided to start an orphanage that would be entirely free of charge, and for which they would never ask any money or support. When they had needs, they would go to God alone, trusting that He would give them everything they needed.

Many people were incredulous, and so the Muellers' purpose in starting the orphanage became twofold: The first was obviously to help the orphans; the second was to show people what it looked like to trust God for *everything*.

When the first orphan house opened, George and his wife, Mary, prayed for everything they needed. According to George's meticulous records, God provided all that they asked for. By the time George died, in 1898, over ten thousand orphans had been housed and cared for in the five orphan houses they built.

During his lifetime, a million and a half pounds went through George's hands in the form of donations. He directed every cent toward those in need. After his death, a British paper wrote of George that he "robbed the cruel streets of thousands of victims, the jails of thousands of felons, and the poorhouses of thousands of helpless waifs."[18] Another newspaper noted that it had all been accomplished by prayer alone.

## Brother Yun

Yun was born in 1958 in the southern part of the Henan Province in China. When he was sixteen years old, with his father dying from stomach and lung cancer and his family nearly starving, Yun met Jesus Christ.

Over the years Yun grew and began to preach the gospel all over the country. The police were constantly tracking him and arrested him more than thirty times. Usually he was able to escape or elude long-term prison stays, but not always. Yun was imprisoned for three lengthy terms, including a four-year term during which he fasted from water and food for a period of seventy-four days. Although it is considered medically impossible for someone to survive that long without water, God sustained him. During those four years he underwent intense torture, including repeated beatings with a whip and multiple shocks from an electric baton.

Later on, Yun was held in a maximum-security prison in Zhengzhou. To ensure that he would never escape their prison, the guards beat Yun's legs until he was crippled. Despite this, Brother Yun walked out of the prison six weeks later. Gates and barriers that were always closed and barred were miraculously opened. No guard tried to stop him; it was as though he were invisible to them. It wasn't until he was outside and safe that Brother Yun realized he was walking on his "broken" legs!

Brother Yun and his family came to Germany in September 2001 after escaping China, where Yun is still wanted by the police. They now encourage believers around the world by sharing what God has done and is doing in China and many other places.

They are deeply involved with Back to Jerusalem, a movement aiming "to preach the gospel and establish fellowships of believers in all the countries, cities, towns, and ethnic groups between China and Jerusalem. This vision is no small task, for within those nations lay the three largest spiritual strongholds in the world today that have yet to be conquered by the gospel: the giants of Islam, Buddhism, and Hinduism."[19]

## Shane Claiborne

Shane is in his late twenties and lives in The Simple Way community house in one of the worst neighborhoods in Philadelphia.

Shane and the other residents at The Simple Way work to expose structures that foster poverty and to imagine alternative ways to live. They take Christ's words in Matthew 25:40 literally when He said, "I tell you the truth, whatever you did for one of the least of these brothers of mine, you did for me." Their lives are about loving the very poor and broken in one of America's hardest cities. They do this in their own community as they feed hungry people, spend time with neighborhood children, run a community store, and reclaim decrepit blocks by planting community gardens.

Shane is a speaker at many conferences, churches, and events around the country. In keeping with the hospitality that characterized the early church, Shane stays with families when he agrees to speak. He doesn't ask for a specific honorarium, only that attendees give what they can to help support the ministries at The Simple Way.

When he travels, Shane asks those who hire him to lessen the ecological impact of his travel by biking to work, carpooling, or donating money to a worthy organization. All proceeds from Shane's book, *The Irresistible Revolution*, are given away.

In 2003, Shane went to Baghdad with the Iraq Peace Team (a project of Voices in the Wilderness and Christian Peacemaker Teams) for three weeks. Shane watched the U.S. invasion of Baghdad. While there, he visited the sites of the daily bombings, hospitals where the injured were taken, and families that had been devastated. He also attended worship services with Iraqi believers. To learn more about The Simple Way, visit www.thesimpleway.org.

## The Robynson Family

This family of five, with three kids under the age of ten, chooses to celebrate the birth of Christ in a unique way. On Christmas mornings, instead of focusing on the presents under the tree, they make pancakes, brew an urn of coffee, and head downtown. Once there, they load the coffee and food into the back of a red wagon. Then, with the eager help of their three-year-old, they pull the wagon around the mostly empty streets in search of homeless folks to offer a warm and filling breakfast on Christmas morning.

All three of the Robynson kids look forward to this time of giving a little bit of tangible love to people who otherwise would have been cold and probably without breakfast. Can you think of a better way to start the holiday that celebrates the God who is Love?

## Susan Diego

Now in her late forties, Susan grew up in a home where God was sought, and she has tried to obey Him her whole life. She has served

Him in many ways, including working with high school students in her church youth group and at the public high school; teaching young mothers to be loving parents; raising four children of her own; starting a school; and opening her home as a place of rest for people of all ages and places in life.

When Susan was young, she told God that she would do anything He asked her to, but that she hated speaking in front of people and would prefer it not be that. However, recently Susan felt like God was moving her heart to speak and that she needed to say yes if an opportunity came up.

It did.

During spring break this year, Susan, her husband, and their two youngest children went to Uganda; there, Susan was in charge of leading a conference for the women. This meant speaking to hundreds of women at least ten different times, on numerous topics.

At first the thought of this terrified Susan. In fact, tears still come to her eyes when she talks about it. But she has submitted. She has said yes to God, to the one thing she hoped *never* to do.


## Lucy

If you met Lucy at church, you would probably think she was somebody's innocent, dear grandmother. She is the kind of woman who will come and give you a huge hug and then introduce herself.

You would never guess that Lucy is an ex-prostitute. When she was in her teens and early twenties, drugs and prostitution dominated her life. Through an older Christian woman who reached out to the prostitutes, Lucy met Jesus and her life was completely transformed.

To this day, almost forty years later, Lucy lives near the same streets where she once worked as a prostitute and consistently opens her home to other young women who are caught in prostitution. It is common knowledge on the streets that if you need anything, you can come to Lucy's house. She doesn't have a lot, but her home is always open. Prostitutes, pimps, drug users, dealers, and anyone else who most people avoid—Lucy invites them in. This is her way of loving people who are in desperate need of the hope and love that Lucy found forty years ago.

## Cornerstone Community Church

We started Cornerstone a little over thirteen years ago. The first few years, we gave about 4 percent of our budget away. As the years went by, we gave more and more money away.

This year we committed to giving away 50 percent of our budget. This is because we believe that when Jesus said to "love your neighbor as yourself," He wasn't kidding. If we really want to love our neighbors as ourselves, then it makes sense that we spend at least as much on them as we do on ourselves.

Another manifestation of our desire to love others is our new building plan. Initially, we had a beautiful plan for a new sanctuary that would have cost many millions of dollars. Now, however, we are in the process of getting permits to build an outdoor amphitheater that will seat plenty of people and save us about $20 million.

I'm sure there will be days when it's uncomfortable outside, but there will also be joy in knowing that we're sitting in the cold so that someone else can have a blanket.

↓↑

I hope these life stories have done more than encourage you; I hope they have eliminated every excuse for not living a radical, love-motivated life. I hope they have challenged the multitudes who "feel called to the rich" and ignore the poor. If biblical examples seem unattainable, hopefully these average, everyday people give you hope that you, too, can live a life worth writing about.

# the crux of the matter

By now you're probably wondering, *What in the world does this mean for me?*

After the apostle Peter preached on the day of Pentecost, people "were cut to the heart and said … 'Brothers, what shall we *do?*'" (Acts 2:37). The first church responded with immediate action: repentance, baptism, selling possessions, sharing the gospel.

We respond with words like *Amen, Convicting sermon, Great book* … and then are paralyzed as we try to decipher what God wants of our lives. I concur with Annie Dillard, who once said, "How we live our days is … how we live our lives." We each need to discover for ourselves how to live *this day* in faithful surrender to God as we "continue to work out [our] salvation with fear and trembling" (Phil. 2:12).

Should you put your house on the market today and downsize? Maybe. Should you quit your job? Maybe. Or perhaps God wants you to work harder at your job and be His witness there. Does He want you to move to another city or another country? Maybe. Perhaps He wants you to stay put and open your eyes to the needs of your neighbors. Honestly, it's hard enough for me to discern how to live my own life!

My suggestion as you think, make decisions, and discern how God would have you live is to ask yourself, "Is this the most loving way to do life? Am I loving my neighbor and my God by living where I live, by driving what I drive, by talking how I talk?" I urge you to consider and actually live as though each person you come into contact with is Christ.

Asking and reflecting on these sorts of questions points us in the right direction, but we have to get beyond asking the right questions. We often have "aha!" moments but don't act; in fact, we're famous for it in the church. Remember those retreat highs followed by the inevitable lull? Or the excitement you felt on your first mission trip but forgot shortly after returning home? Memories are wonderful, but do you live differently because of them?

The stories in chapter 9 are brief snapshots of how a few people have lived out true Christianity in America and around the world. Their lives are a challenge of the status quo and examples of a different way to live.

The point is that there *is* another path, an alternative to the individualism, selfishness, and materialism of the American Dream (even the so-called Christian version). I hope their stories reminded you that God works in a vast number of ways, that He has more in store for you than you can really imagine right now.

A Nike commercial ran years ago, featuring the first-draft pick into the NBA, Harold Miner. In the commercial, he said something like, "Some people ask if I'm going to be the next Magic Johnson, the next Larry Bird, or the next Michael Jordan. I tell them, I'm going to be the first Harold Miner." He ended up having a miserable career in the NBA, but it was still a cool commercial. And his point—to be yourself—was valid.

Oswald Chambers writes, "Never make a principle out of your experience; let God be as original with other people as He is with you."[20] To that I would add, "Be careful not to turn others' lives into the mold for your own." Allow God to be as creative with you as He is with each of us.

Have you ever said, "I was made for this moment"? Do you believe you were crafted for specific good works, things that God knew before you even existed? Or do you compare your life to others and lament what you have been given?

We have a God who is a Creator, not a duplicator. He's never made a Francis Chan before. Paul tells us,

> There are different kinds of gifts, but the same Spirit. There are different kinds of service, but the same Lord. There are different kinds of working, but the same God works all of them in all men. Now to each one the manifestation of the Spirit is given for the common good.
>
> —1 Corinthians 12:4–7

Imagine if you opened up a drawer in your kitchen and found twenty cheese graters but no other utensils. Not very helpful when you're looking for something to eat your soup with. Just as there are different utensils in the kitchen that serve diverse functions, God has created unique people to accomplish a variety of purposes throughout the world.

That is why I cannot say in this book, "Everyone is supposed to be a missionary" or "You need to sell your car and start taking public transportation." What I *can* say is that you must learn to listen to and obey God, especially in a society where it's easy and expected to do what is most comfortable.

⇵

I wrote this book because much of our talk doesn't match our lives. We say things like, "I can do all things through Christ who strengthens me," and "Trust in the Lord with all your heart." Then we live and plan like we don't believe God even exists. We try to set our lives up so everything will be fine even if God doesn't come through. But true faith means holding nothing back. It means putting every hope in God's fidelity to His promises.

A friend of mine once said that Christians are like manure: spread them out and they help everything grow better, but keep them in one big pile and they stink horribly. Which are you? The kind that reeks, around which people walk a wide swath? Or the kind that trusts God enough to let Him spread you out—whether that means going outside your normal group of Christian friends, increasing your material giving, or using your time to serve others?

I was convicted by my lack of faith in college. I realized that my choices had situated me in a pile of stinking manure, and this motivated me to put myself in uncomfortable situations. I began going into downtown Los Angeles to share my faith. I didn't "hear God calling me" to drive downtown; I just chose to go. I obeyed.

Most of us use "I'm waiting for God to reveal His calling on my life" as a means of avoiding action. Did you hear God calling you to sit in front of the television yesterday? Or to go on your last vacation? Or exercise this morning? Probably not, but you still did it. The point isn't that vacations or exercise are wrong, but that we are quick to rationalize our entertainment and priorities yet are slow to commit to serving God.

A friend of mine was speaking recently. Afterward a guy came up and told him, "I would go serve God as a missionary overseas, but, honestly, if I went right now it would only be out of obedience." My friend's response was "Yes, and …?"

Jesus said, "If you love me, you will obey what I command" (John 14:15). Jesus did not say, "If you love me you will obey me when you feel called or good about doing so …" If we love, then we obey. Period. This sort of matter-of-fact obedience is part of what it means to live a life of faith.

The greatest blessing I received during those trips to the inner city was seeing God work in situations where He has to. As a result, I've made it a commitment to consistently put myself in situations that scare me and require God to come through. When I survey my life, I realize that *those* times have been the most meaningful and satisfying of my life. They were the times when I truly experienced life and God.

↓↑

For so much of my life I didn't understand the desirability of God or trust in His love enough to submit my hopes and dreams. I lived in a constant state of trying to be "devoted enough" to Him, yet I never quite made it.

I knew God wanted all of me, yet I feared what complete surrender to Him would mean. Trying harder doesn't work for me. Slowly I've learned to pray for God's help, and He has become my greatest love and desire.

Despite this huge shift in focus and tone in my relationship with God, I still struggle to stay focused on Jesus every day. But a couple of things help me keep going.

First, I remember that if I stop pursuing Christ, I am letting our relationship deteriorate. We never grow closer to God when we just live life; it takes deliberate pursuit and attentiveness. When I pray, I sometimes ask God to make it the most intimate time of prayer I've *ever* had. Many times when I speak, whether at my church or another venue, I remind myself that I could die right after I finish, so what would I want my last words to be?

Second, I remember that we are not alone. Even now there are thousands of beings in heaven watching what is going on down here—a "great cloud of witnesses," the Scripture says. It reminds me that there is so much more to our existence than what we can see. What we do reverberates through the heavens and into eternity.

Try for a whole day to be conscious of heaven. Realize that so much is going on outside of this dimension and our existence. God and His angels are watching, even now.

What really keeps me going is the gift and power we have been given in the Holy Spirit. Before Christ left this earth, He told His disciples,

> I tell you the truth: It is for your good that I am going away. Unless I go away, the Counselor will not come to you; but if I go, I will send him to you. When he comes, he will convict the world of guilt in regard to sin and righteousness and judgment.… When he, the Spirit of truth, comes, he will guide you into all truth.
>
> —John 16:7–8, 13

The disciples must have been shocked by the idea that it was for their good that Jesus was leaving. What could possibly be better than having Jesus by your side? Wouldn't you rather have Jesus physically walking next to you all day than have the seemingly elusive Holy Spirit living in you?

Our view of the Holy Spirit is too small. The Holy Spirit is the One who changes the church, but we have to remember that the Holy Spirit lives in us. It is individual people living Spirit-filled lives that will change the church.

Ephesians 5:18 says, "Be filled with the Spirit." If you look at the Greek, it is written as both a present imperative (a continual command)

and in the passive voice. The imperative part means that being filled with the Spirit isn't something we do once; rather, it is something we do always and repeatedly. And the passive element communicates God's necessary action in the process of filling.

I have never been more excited about the church. I think there is tremendous reason to expect good things. At the beginning of this chapter, I mentioned how Annie Dillard wrote that the way we live out our days is the way we will live our lives. It's similar with the body of Christ: How we believers live out our lives is a microcosm of the life of the church.

My hope and prayer is that you finish this book with hope, believing that part of your responsibility in the body of Christ is to help set the pace for the church by listening and obeying and *living* Christ. Knowing that God has called us each to live faithful and devoted lives before Him, by the power of His Spirit. You do not need to preach to your pastor or congregation; you simply need to live out in your daily life the love and obedience that God has asked of you.

I was recently told about a man who heard me preach on 1 Corinthians 15:19–20, where Paul writes, "If only for this life we have hope in Christ, we are to be pitied more than all men. But Christ has indeed been raised from the dead." This man was convicted that since Christ is indeed alive, he needed to live like it. So he quit his well-paying job and became a pastor—something he had felt called to do for a while.

When people make changes in their lives like this, it carries greater impact than when they merely make impassioned declarations. The world needs Christians who don't tolerate the complacency of their own lives.

## Is This What I Want to Be Doing When Christ Comes Back?

And so we are at the end of this book. I don't think it's coincidence that God has encouraged my heart so much over this past week with the story of the three believers who were martyred in Turkey.

I'm writing this in April 2007, and the news about the three martyrs—Tilman, Necati, and Ugur—is still fresh. I can't get them out of my mind. They were tortured for three hours in ways that I didn't know were humanly possible. I'll spare you the details, but it was repulsive and horrific. I think of how they must have looked at each other while being tortured with stares that said, "Just hold on a little longer. Don't deny Him! It'll all be worth it."

It's been about a week and a half since their deaths. How thrilled they must be right now—I cannot imagine the joy they felt just five seconds after their deaths. I know that when I meet them, they'll say it was so worth it. A hundred or thousand or million years from now, they'll still say it was so incredibly worth it. Stories about faithful saints like our brothers killed in Turkey are what we will talk about in heaven.

The Bible is clear that each of us will stand before God and account for our lives:

> For we must all appear before the judgment seat of Christ, so that each one may receive what is due for what he has done in the body, whether good or evil. (2 Cor. 5:10 ESV)

O great and mighty God, whose name is the LORD of hosts
… rewarding each one according to his ways and according
to the fruit of his deeds. (Jer. 32:18–19 ESV)

For we will all stand before the judgment seat of God; for
it is written, "As I live, says the Lord, every knee shall bow
to me, and every tongue shall confess to God." So then each
of us will give an account of himself to God. (Rom.
14:10–12 ESV)

What will people say about your life in heaven? Will people speak of
God's work and glory through you? And even more important, how
will you answer the King when He says, "What did you do with what
I gave you?"

Daniel Webster once said, "The greatest thought that has ever
entered my mind is that one day I will have to stand before a holy God
and give an account of my life." He was right.

Now close this book. Get on your knees before our holy, loving God.
And then live the life with your friends, your family, parents, spouse,
children, neighbors, enemies, and strangers that He has created and
empowered you through the Holy Spirit to live.

May you be able to say at the end of your life, along with Paul,

I have fought the good fight, I have finished the race, I
have kept the faith. Henceforth there is laid up for me the

crown of righteousness, which the Lord, the righteous judge, will award to me on that Day, and not only to me but also to all who have loved his appearing.

—2 Timothy 4:7–8 ESV

# NOTES

1. R. C. Sproul, *The Holiness of God* (Carol Stream, IL: Tyndale House, 2000), 68.

2. A. W. Tozer, *The Knowledge of the Holy* (San Francisco: HarperSanFrancisco, 1992), 1.

3. Frederick Buechner, *The Hungering Dark* (New York: HarperOne, 1985), 72.

4. Wikipedia, s.v. "world population," http://en.wikipedia.org/wiki/world_population.

5. Frederic D. Huntington, *Forum* magazine, 1890.

6. David Goetz, *Death by Suburb* (New York: HarperOne, 2007), 9.

7. Robert Murray M'Cheyne, as quoted in John Piper, *Don't Waste Your Life* (Wheaton, IL: Crossway, 2003), 105.

8. Mark Buchanan, *The Rest of God* (Nashville: Thomas Nelson Publishers, 2007), 158.

9. Henri Nouwen, *With Open Hands* (Notre Dame, IN: Ave Maria Press, 2006), 65.

10. A. W. Tozer, The *Pursuit of God* (Camp Hill, PA: WingSpread, 2007).

11. John Piper, *God Is the Gospel* (Wheaton, IL: Crossway, 2005), 15.

12. David Livingston (speech, Cambridge University, Cambridge, England, December 4, 1857).

13. Attributed to Matthew Henry.

14. *The American Heritage Dictionary of the English Language*, 4th ed. (New York: Houghton Mifflin Company, 2004), s.v. "obsessed."

15. See www.familyresource.com.

16. See www.mossyfoot.com.

17. See www.standwithafrica.org.

18. Janet Benge, *George Mueller: Guardian of Bristol's Orphans* (Seattle: YWAM, 1999), 196.

19. See www.backtojerusalem.com.

20. Oswald Chambers, *My Utmost for His Highest*, June 13 entry.

# A CONVERSATION WITH FRANCIS CHAN

**Q: Tell us about the title *Crazy Love*.**

A: The idea of *Crazy Love* has to do with our relationship with God. All my life I've heard people say, "God loves you." It's probably the most insane statement you could make to say that the eternal Creator of this universe is in love with me. There is a response that ought to take place in believers, a crazy reaction to that love. Do you really understand what God has done for you? If so, why is your response so lukewarm?

**Q: The emergent movement calls for a change in the church. How is your message and approach different?**

A: As a pastor I hear a lot of emergent leaders talk about what is wrong with the church. It comes across as someone who doesn't love the church. I'm a pastor first and foremost, and I'm trying to offer a solution or a model of what church should look like. I'm going back to Scripture and seeing what the church was in its simplest form and trying to re-create that in my own church. I'm not coming up with anything new. I'm calling people to go back to the way it was. I'm not bashing the church. I'm loving it.

**Q: Why do you think so many Christians blame the church for their failures?**

A: We all need to justify our actions. The easiest thing to do when we're not living how God wants us to is to blame someone or something else. It's not unique to the church. You see it everywhere, people blaming their parents, a chemical imbalance, whatever, rather than looking to themselves and changing who they are through the Holy Spirit. The same thing happens in the church. All of us who have the Holy Spirit have the potential to live a "crazy love" type of life, but it's easier to not live it and blame someone for that.

**Q: You talk about believing in God without having a clue what He's like. As a Christian, how is that possible?**

A: Because we're taught so little about God, most people just want to know what God can do for them rather than desiring to know Him. When we present the gospel, we try to answer one question: How do I keep from going to hell? After that question is answered, we stop asking questions about God. With the American church being so concerned about converts, we don't take the time to present the God-centered universe to people. We don't try to dig deep into the truth of God. We need to learn the attributes of God before we know what He is like.

**Q: What is a "giving church"? How do you practice this in your own church? Why do you think it's important for the American church to get to this point?**

A: To me, this has been the greatest thing for our church. I've seen God come through so many times in my personal life when I'm giving. With the church, we weren't as giving as I was personally. I would always ask: God, are You really gonna come through for the church? I wanted to put the message of love your neighbor as yourself into action. It's been an experiment and a step of faith. Cornerstone Community Church has been giving away 55 percent of everything that comes in and things are healthier than ever.

We committed one million dollars to Children's Hunger Fund with payments of $250,000 every three months. During the summer, our funds were lean. I was thinking, *Where are we going to come up with the money for Children's Hunger Fund?* I didn't make a plea during the offering or mention our situation to the congregation. That Sunday, we had an offering of $251,000. It was immediate affirmation that God is saying, "This is exactly what I want you to do." It lifts the faith of all of our people, and our church has seen the hand of God. That's why I think it's so great to be a giving church.

**Q: There is urgency in your message. Where does this come from?**

A: I think from two things. One, I'm doing funerals just about every week. A lot of these funerals are people younger than I am, and so many of them are unexpected. Seeing the shock of their loved ones and realizing God can take your life at any time gives me a sense of urgency.

The other is my upbringing. My mom died giving birth to me; my stepmom died when I was nine; my dad died when I was twelve. I learned that there might not be a tomorrow. I always want this to be the greatest message I'll preach in case I'm not here to give another one.

I have a sense of urgency built into me from my upbringing and going to so many funerals and seeing friends pass away. I can't help but be urgent in my message.

**Q: You talk about what it means to be a lukewarm Christian. You make a bold statement that "churchgoers who are 'lukewarm' are not Christians. We will not see them in heaven." How do you explain this? How does grace play into this statement?**

A: I explain it through the passage of Revelation 3 and look at the passage objectively. God says that the lukewarm will be spit out of His mouth, and that is drastically different than God embracing you and welcoming you into heaven. The lukewarm still need to be saved. How can we say a lukewarm Christian is saved?

Salvation has nothing to do with my performance. If I'm truly saved, then my actions are going to show. All through the New Testament a person's faith is shown through his actions. New Testament teachings are clear that someone who loves God and doesn't obey God is a liar, and the truth is not in Him.

It's not popular to question someone's actions and salvation, and Scripture tells us to test ourselves and see if we're really in the faith. I believe 100 percent in grace, that I did nothing, and I'm completely saved by the cross. By the grace of God we believe and are saved. If someone has the Holy Spirit in them, there will be fruit, and there will not be a lukewarm life.

**Q: Talk about living "your best life later."**

A: It's all about heaven. Hebrews 11 is all about martyrs who never got to see or experience the fulfillment until afterward. Scripture talks about life after this one. We're supposed to be storing treasures in heaven. Why would we store up things on earth? It's an issue of faith. There are very few Christians who say they don't believe in heaven, but their actions show that they don't. If we really believe that if we sacrifice things on earth so that we will have an eternity of rewards, it's the only thing that makes sense.

**Q: In one chapter you state, "Dare to imagine what it would mean for you to take the words of Jesus seriously." What does this mean? Why do you think so many Christians would turn down this dare?**

A: We've conditioned ourselves to hear messages without responding. Sermons have become Christian entertainment. We go to church to hear a well-developed sermon and a convicting thought. We've trained ourselves to believe that if we're convicted, our job is done. If you're just hearing the Word and not actually doing something with it, you're deceiving yourself.

I remember preaching on Luke 6, and I brought up the passage that says, "Do good to those who hate you." I told the congregation to think of someone who hated them, and I asked, "Are you willing to go do something good for them? Will you do that? Yes or no?" I said, "Tell God right now, 'No I will not do that.'" We're not willing to make that statement because we don't want to say that to God, but we're doing that every day.

We don't think it through because we've developed a habit of listening to the Word of God and not obeying it. If we take Scripture literally and if we actually apply it, we won't have what our flesh desires, so we walk away sad or we run to the church where no one else is doing it, but they seem okay with that.

**Q: What do you tell people who say that you are taking the Bible too literally?**

A: If someone told me that I took the Bible too literally, I would really get them to question their own heart. I would ask them if they really believed that we're not supposed to take it that literally, or if it's the influence of other believers who say we're not supposed to. I like to get people to think for themselves and not just go with the flow. When believers are alone with the Word, they come to the same conclusion that I do. *Crazy Love* appeals to thoughts that all Christians have had when they're alone with God, and they realize that they are supposed to take Scripture literally. These are the things they should do.

**Q: How does the American dream play into a lukewarm faith?**

A: It's interesting when we talk about the American dream. In Luke 12, Jesus tells the parable of the rich fool. There's this guy who is rich and has an abundance of crops. He builds bigger barns so that he can store it up. He says, "[I] have plenty of good things laid up for many years. Take life easy; eat, drink, and be merry." Basically, he'll retire and enjoy himself, the American dream. God says, "You fool! This very night your life will be demanded from you."

We shouldn't worry about our lives, what we'll eat, buy, or wear. God says the American dream is absolute foolishness. It's exactly what Christians are doing and defending. God could take your life at any time. Don't conform to the patterns of this world.

**Q: Do you think God calls you to live a radical, crazy life?**

A: It's not that this lifestyle should be crazy to us. It should be the only thing that makes sense. Giving up everything and sacrificing everything we can for the afterlife is logical. "Crazy" is living a safe life and storing up things while trying to enjoy our time on earth, knowing that any millisecond God could take your life. To me that is crazy, and that is radical. The crazy ones are the ones who live life like there is no God. To me that is insanity.

# ABOUT THE COAUTHOR

Danae Yankoski graduated from Westmont College, where she studied English Literature and met her best friend, now husband, Mike. She published her first book at age sixteen, and has since been part of several writing projects. Some of Danae's favorite aspects of life include steaming mugs of tea; hiking, running, and being outside; thought-provoking conversations; interacting with different cultures; and playing with her new black Lab puppy, Elliott. She and Mike recently spent several months living in African and South American communities affected by a lack of clean water. Their heart is to write about these experiences in a way that moves readers beyond statistics, to truly loving their neighbors as themselves.

Also available from Francis Chan and David C. Cook:

# CHAPTER 6

## Forget About His Will for Your Life!

*And to expose our hearts to truth and consistently*
*refuse or neglect to obey the impulses it arouses*
*is to stymie the motions of life within us and, if*
*persisted in, to grieve the Holy Spirit into silence.*

-A.W. Tozer-

How many times have you heard someone say, "I just wish I knew God's will for my life"? I know I've longed for this before. But now I see it as a misguided way of thinking and talking.

There are very few people in the Scriptures who received their life plan from God in advance (or even their five-year plan, for that matter!). Consider Abraham, who was told to pack up his family and all his possessions and start walking. He didn't know where he was going. He didn't know if he would ever be back. He didn't know any of the details we consider vital (e.g., his destination, how long the venture would take, what the costs/rewards would be, whether he'd receive a 401(k) or health insurance). God said to go and he went, and that's pretty much all he knew.

I think a lot of us need to forget about *God's will for my life*. God cares more about our response to His Spirit's leading today, in this moment, than about what we intend to do next year. In fact, the decisions we make next year will be profoundly affected by the degree to which we submit to the Spirit right now, in today's decisions.

It is easy to use the phrase "God's will for my life" as an excuse for inaction or even disobedience. It's much less demanding to think about God's will for your future than it is to ask Him what He wants you to do in the next ten minutes. It's safer to commit to following Him *someday* instead of this day.

To be honest, I believe part of the desire to "know God's will for my life" is birthed in fear and results in paralysis. We are scared to make mistakes, so we fret over figuring out God's will. We wonder what living according to His will would actually look and feel like, and we are scared to find out. We forget that we were never promised a twenty-year plan of action; instead, God promises multiple times in Scripture never to leave or forsake us.

God wants us to listen to His Spirit on a daily basis, and even throughout the day, as difficult and stretching moments arise, and in the midst of the mundane. My hope is that instead of searching for

"God's will for my life," each of us would learn to seek hard after "the Spirit's leading in my life today." May we learn to pray for an open and willing heart, to surrender to the Spirit's leading with that friend, child, spouse, circumstance, or decision in our lives right now.

To say that we are not called to figure out "God's will for my life" does not mean God doesn't have purposes and plans for each of our lives or that He doesn't care what we do with our lives. He does. In both the Old and New Testaments He tells us that this is true. The key is that He never promises to reveal these purposes all at once, in advance.

We do know that we are called to keep in step with the Holy Spirit. In Paul's letter to the Galatians we read, "But I say, walk by the Spirit, and you will not gratify the desires of the flesh.... If we live by the Spirit, let us also walk by the Spirit" (5:16, 25).

The phrases *keeping in step with the Spirit* and *walking with the Spirit* are mostly likely familiar, but do they affect your life in a practical and meaningful way? Like I said earlier, I think dwelling on God's plan for the future often excuses us from faithful and sacrificial living now. It tends to create a safe zone of sorts, where we can sit around and have "spiritual" conversations about what God "might" have planned for our lives. Thinking, questioning, and talking can take the place of letting the Spirit affect our immediate actions in radical ways. God wants to see His children stake everything on His power and presence in their lives.

Nowhere in Scripture do I see a "balanced life with a little bit of God added in" as an ideal for us to emulate. Yet when I look at our churches, this is exactly what I see: a lot of people who have added Jesus to their lives. People who have, in a sense, asked Him to join them on *their* life journey, to follow *them* wherever *they* feel they should go, rather than following Him as we are commanded. The God of the universe is not something we can just add to our lives and keep on as we did before. The Spirit who raised Christ from the dead is not someone we can just call on when we want a little extra power in our lives. Jesus Christ did not die in order to follow *us*. He died and rose again so that we could forget everything else and follow Him to the cross, to true Life.

<hr />

When people give their lives to God in exchange for a ticket out of hell, there is often no turning or change of direction, which is the definition of repentance. If all you want is a little Jesus to "spiritualize" your life, a little extra God to keep you out of hell, you are missing out on the fullness of life you were created for.

Not only this, you don't need the Holy Spirit. You don't need the Holy Spirit if you are merely seeking to live a semi-moral life and attend church regularly. You can find people of all sorts in many religions doing that quite nicely without Him. You only need the Holy Spirit's guidance and help if you truly want to follow the Way of Jesus Christ. You only need Him if you desire to "obey everything" He commanded and to teach others to do the same (Matt. 28:18–20 NIV). You only need the Holy Spirit if you have genuinely repented and believe. And you only need the Holy Spirit if you understand that you are called to share in Christ's suffering and death, as well as

His resurrection (Rom. 8:17; 2 Cor. 4:16–18; Phil. 3:10–11). Paul demonstrated this when he wrote,

> But we have this treasure in jars of clay to show that this all-surpassing power is from God and not from us. We are hard pressed on every side, but not crushed; perplexed, but not in despair; persecuted, but not abandoned; struck down, but not destroyed. We always carry around in our body the death of Jesus, so that the life of Jesus may also be revealed in our body. For we who are alive are always being given over to death for Jesus' sake, so that his life may also be revealed in our mortal body. (2 Cor. 4:7–11 NIV)

If you truly believe and have turned from the way you were headed and joined a different Way of living, then you desperately need the Holy Spirit. You know you cannot live this Way without the Spirit in you.

I think repentance is one of those words we hear a lot but maybe don't incorporate into our lives very often. When I use the word repent, I think about the time I was in a dating relationship, until one day a girl named Lisa came to my church as a guest soloist and caught my attention. After getting to know her, I knew she was the one I wanted to be with. I didn't consider it an option to ask Lisa if she wanted to date me also. I knew I had to break off the other relationship if I wanted to begin one with Lisa.

In a sense, this is what repentance is like when we meet Jesus: We totally change direction.

Some people encounter Jesus and say, "Sweet! Jesus, do You want to join the party of my life with this sin, that addiction, this destructive relationship, and we'll all just coexist together?" But repentance means saying, "Sweet Jesus, You are the best thing that has ever happened to me! I want to turn from all the sin and selfishness that rules me. I want to let it go and walk with You. Only You. You are my life now. Help me to walk away from the enslaving, worthless things in life."

Do you see the difference between these two examples? Which do you think more accurately portrays your own life? Is there anything you need to go and make right with your Savior, the One who was killed for your sake? If so, don't hesitate to shut this book and spend the necessary time. Nothing else matters more than this relationship.

---

So if a little bit of spirituality added in to our lives is not what God has in mind, what does He want for His children? How does He desire that we live? The fact is we were called by Jesus to give up everything. His call is to come and take up the cross (Luke 9:23).

"Taking up my cross" has become a euphemism for getting through life's typical burdens with a semi-good attitude. Yet life's typical burdens—busy schedules, bills, illness, hard decisions, paying for college tuition, losing jobs, houses not selling, and the family dog dying—are felt by everyone, whether or not they follow the Way of Jesus.

When Jesus calls us to take up our cross, He is doing much more than calling us to endure the daily, circumstantial troubles of life. The people in Jesus' day were very familiar with the cross. Having witnessed crucifixion, they understood the commitment and sacrifice of taking up a cross.

It is a call to radical faith.

Jesus is calling us to be willing to suffer anything and forsake everything for the sake of the gospel. His call is to love those who have cheated us in business; those who have spread nasty rumors about us; those who would kill us if they could; those who disagree with us politically, practically, and fundamentally. His call is to consider everything a loss for His sake. His call is for total surrender. He calls us to give up all that we have, to give even to the point of offering up our lives as a living sacrifice. His call means realizing that His power is made perfect in our weakness, that when we are weak we are also strong (2 Cor. 12:9–10).

Do you remember the story where Jesus saw people putting gifts into the offering box? At first some rich people gave, and it sounds like their contributions must have been monetarily large. Then Jesus pointed out a widow (the text even says a "poor widow") who put in two small copper coins. Notice Christ's words in response to what he witnessed: "Truly, I tell you, this poor widow has put in more than all of them. For they all contributed out of their abundance, but she out of her poverty put in all she had to live on" (Luke 21:3–4). Jesus commends this woman, whom the world—those people with power and money—overlooked and perhaps even derided. Jesus praises her for her revolutionary faith, for holding nothing back. She literally gave everything she had, even though she was a "poor widow" with no other means of income or support. And Jesus holds her up as an example.

What if you could hear the voice of the Holy Spirit and He asked you to literally give everything you owned? What if He asked you to sell all your possessions and give the money to the poor? Could you do it? Before you start explaining why He would never ask that of you, take a moment and answer the question honestly. It's not out of His character to ask for everything.

I don't know about you, but that challenges me like crazy. I say I want to give it all to God, to truly submit myself to the leading of the Holy Spirit. But I won't lie; sometimes the reality of what that means leaves me wanting to hold back a little. There are things on this earth that I really enjoy, like surfing, golfing, eating out, and laughing with friends. I know what you're thinking: that those things are not sinful. And you are right. But that doesn't mean the Spirit will not lead me to forgo those things occasionally or maybe even permanently for His purposes and the glory of the Father.

I struggle to always and actually keep in step with the Spirit moment by moment. To submit and give up everything truly is radical and terrifying. However, when I think deeply about it, walking in my own wisdom, contrary to the Spirit's leading, is even more frightful. Though I struggle, I know that ultimately I want nothing more than to live in total surrender and abandonment to the Spirit every moment I have left on this earth.

The Spirit may lead me into total sacrifice financially, or He may lead me toward humiliation in the opinions of people around me.

The Spirit may ask me to move to a different city, a different state, or a different country. The Spirit may ask me to stay where I am and spend my time in very different ways than I do now. He could lead me toward actions like in 2 Samuel 6, where David danced (it says in "a linen ephod," the equivalent of priestly underwear) before the Lord "with all his might" (v. 14). Others were shamed by his undignified display of worship to God, yet David said that he didn't care and that he would become even more undignified for the sake of the Lord. All he cared about was worshipping his God.

When I read this story, part of me says, "Yes, I want to live like David. I want to forget about what others think and worship my King with all of me." The other part of me says, "Okay, but practically, what does that look like?" How do I walk in such intimacy with the Spirit that my genuine response when He moves is to dance with abandon, heedless of those around me who might consider it inappropriate? And do I really need not to care about what others think of me?

The crux of it, I believe, is realizing that being filled with the Spirit is not a one-time act. As we read in Galatians about the Spirit and the flesh, walking with the Spirit implies an ongoing relationship. Being filled with the Spirit is not limited to the day we first meet Christ. Instead, throughout Scripture we read of a relationship that calls us into an active pursuit of the Spirit.

Christians can't ever lose the Spirit, but His filling is something we should constantly pursue. This business of sanctification is a lifelong process we are engaged in. Second Corinthians 3:18 says, "We all, who with unveiled faces contemplate the Lord's glory, are being transformed into his image with ever-increasing glory, which comes from the Lord, who is the Spirit" (TNIV). (See also 2 Thess. 2:13 and Rom. 15:16.)

Imagine I buy a treadmill to lose some weight. Three months later I take it back to the store and complain to the clerk that it didn't work—I didn't lose a pound. He asks me, "What was the problem? Did it not work properly?" I respond, "I don't know if it works. I never ran on it. I just know I didn't lose any weight, so I am done with it!"

This may seem like a silly example, but change the details and suddenly it sounds pretty familiar:

"I have prayed for the Holy Spirit to free me from my lust, and I am still addicted to pornography." Or, "I have prayed for years to be able to forgive my dad, but I am still racked with anger and bitterness thirty years down the road." "I have prayed for years to be free of my gluttony, but despite prayer, spiritually based support groups, and dieting, I am still a compulsive, unhealthy eater." Fill in whatever sin plagues you and suddenly the treadmill illustration doesn't seem so silly. In fact, it seems like those prayers for freedom from that ongoing sin didn't really "work" in much the same way the treadmill didn't help me lose any weight.

Receiving freedom and healing in answer to prayer is generally not something that is done to you, a situation in which you are just a passive participant. Occasionally God works this way and simply heals or frees a person outright. He is certainly capable of this. But in my experience, He typically asks us to play an active role in the journey toward wholeness. He doesn't need our help but invites us to participate. Often this journey to freedom takes time, sometimes a very long time. And it takes perseverance. It takes participation on our part. We have to get on the treadmill and run—merely looking at the workout machine doesn't do a whole lot. (See also Rom. 12:11 and 1 Thess. 5:19.)

Have you been stuck in a cycle of sin for a long time? Have you given up on the Holy Spirit and resigned yourself to thinking that He doesn't "work" or doesn't have the power to bring freedom, at least not in your life? If this is you, then maybe you have not internalized the reality that walking in the Spirit requires action on your part.

Because the fact is that if you were in step with the Holy Spirit, listening to and obeying Him, you wouldn't sin (Gal. 5:16). In any given moment, it is impossible to live in the power of the Spirit and sin at the same time. Sin is wholly opposed to everything that is of the Spirit. They really are mutually exclusive and totally contrary to each other.

This does not mean that if you sin, you don't have the Holy Spirit or aren't a follower of Christ. It does mean that when you are sinning, you are not simultaneously submitted to the authority and presence of the Holy Spirit in your life. He is still present, but you are most likely suppressing or ignoring His counsel.

The hopeful part in all this is that even when we do ignore the Spirit and sin, the Holy Spirit convicts us of that sin. Though at times we sin, we are not ruled and enslaved by sin as we once were. We have cut off the headship of sin in our lives. When we are attuned to the Spirit, we are reminded of this freeing reality.

It's obvious when someone is not walking in the Spirit (at least not consistently). What you see and experience from such a person is usually along the lines of rage, selfishness, dissension, bitterness, and envy. However, when a person is habitually and actively submitted to the Spirit, what comes out of his or her life is the fruit of the Spirit. The Holy Spirit will not—cannot—lead you into sin. If the Holy Spirit is in you, as a believer, then when you sin you are not listening to the Spirit's leading.

---

Haven't you met those rare people who you can tell are daily keeping in step with the Spirit? Somehow they exude graciousness and peacefulness to a degree that is not humanly possible. Don't you want that in your own life? I mean, who really wants to be a stressed-out, angry, selfish person? It's not much fun, for you or anyone who happens to come in contact with you.

Several people in my own life come to mind when I think about people who walk with the Spirit daily. It would be easy to start comparing ourselves to others in this area. I can already hear the thought progression: *Well, I am obviously more Spirit-led than* that *person....*

Instead of wasting time deliberating over whether others are walking with the Spirit (which is definitely not our job), I challenge you to examine yourself. Look at the "fruit" of your own life and let it be a gauge for you of your own connectedness with the Spirit. Do you listen to the Holy Spirit as you stand in line at the post office? Perhaps He is asking you to begin a conversation with the elderly lady in front of you. Do you allow the Holy Spirit to lead when you are making your budget? Perhaps He will direct you to allocate the monies differently than you otherwise would. Do you submit to the Holy Spirit as you spend time with your family? Often it is family members who are most difficult to love, and we need the Spirit's help to love them well. These are just a few of the many, many areas of our lives that we can submit to the Spirit's leading. Take some time to think about areas in your own life where you tend just to do your own thing, heedless of the Spirit's will and call.

Living by the Spirit implies a habitual, continual, and active interaction with the Holy Spirit. While this sounds exhausting, it really isn't because all of this living and action is done in the power of the Spirit. It is not by your own strength.

This, however, brings up a whole other confusing issue: Is it God's work or my work? God's responsibility or mine? Paul addresses this when he writes to the Galatians. He calls them out, asking whom they had been bewitched by (quite an accusation!). He asks, "Having begun by the Spirit, are you now being perfected by the flesh?" (3:3).

I think each of us has a strong tendency to attempt to wrestle control from the Spirit and "do" this life on our own. Each of us tends to switch from living the gospel of grace to trusting in a system of works. That's why Paul brings up this issue with the churches in Galatia. He knows it's hard to truly depend on sustenance and

guidance from the Spirit rather than merely on our own wisdom
and effort.

Remember the treadmill illustration? Perhaps you wonder how
the concept of our actions fits in with the gospel of grace, which
cannot be merited or earned. Suppose I bake a loaf of bread and you
asked me, "Which ingredient is more important, the yeast or the
flour?" I would look at my still-warm loaf of bread and reply that
both are fundamentally necessary to the making of bread; you simply
would not have bread without both yeast and flour.

This illustration bears a similarity to our spiritual lives. If we
never responded to God, if we never acted based on what He has
done for us, there wouldn't be much of a relationship there. God is
still real and moving, but at some point we have to respond and act
because of what He's done. Like yeast and flour are both necessary
to bread, both God's action and our response-action are necessary in
this relationship with God.

In the book of Philippians, Paul writes, "Therefore, my beloved,
as you have always obeyed, so now, not only as in my presence but
much more in my absence, work out your own salvation with fear and
trembling, for it is God who works in you, both to will and to work
for his good pleasure" (2:12–13). I love the apparent contradiction in
this passage. Paul says in one breath, "Work out your own salvation,"
and in the next, "It is God who works in you." The both-ness here
doesn't allow us to escape with a simple conclusion. Yes, it is God
who works in you. And, yes, there is work for you to do. Yes, the
Spirit empowers you to do the work. And, yes, you do the work.

Like many things in life, there really isn't a sew-it-all-up
solution. And I love that. God is big and mysterious enough that we

cannot simply put a label on this process and move on. It requires continual engagement and wrestling and discovering how to live a Spirit-filled life today. Not ten years from now. Not tomorrow. But right now, in the particular time and place He has put us. As we "work out our salvation" and as "God works in us." Let us keep in step.

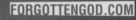